Eggs, Omelets & Quiche

Checkerboard Cookbooks

NEW YORK

Adapted from *Le Uova*, by Lorenza Stucchi, in the series ''Jolly
della Buona Cucina'' (Series Editor, Luigi Carnacina; Photographs
by Mario Metteucci, Sandro Pagani, and Romano Vada)

First published in USA 1982 by Checkerboard Cookbooks
Checkerboard Cookbooks is a trademark of Simon & Schuster, Inc.
Distributed by Bookthrift, New York, NY

Editorial adaptation and production by
Accolade Books, Inc., New York, NY

Editorial director: John Kremitske
Editorial consultant: Nancy Parilla Macagno
Recipe editing and adaptation: Pam Rabin, Dale McAdoo
Introduction by: Stephen Schmidt
Layout: Marcia Rizzi
Cover design: Michael Simon

ISBN 0-89673-116-2

Printed in Italy

Introduction

Facts About Eggs and Their Uses

NUTRITIONAL VALUE AND COMMERCIAL GRADES

Eggs are a truly universal food. Consumed by human beings down through the ages, eggs have evolved continuously in endless appetizing and favorite dishes, prepared in countless ways and varying textures throughout the world. In one form or another, they can be served at any meal of the day—in appetizers, soups, main courses, side dishes, or desserts—and for snacks in between as well.

Eggs are widely considered to provide the best animal protein in the human diet. Egg protein is of such high quality that it is often used as a natural standard by which all other protein values are measured. Eggs are an excellent source of vitamins, particularly A and D, plus many nourishing minerals. An average-size egg contains about 85 calories, with a little over three-quarters of the calorie count being attributable to the yolk.

The size of eggs is customarily determined by their weight by the dozen. Jumbo eggs weigh 30 ounces per dozen; Extra Large, 27 ounces; Large, 24 ounces; Medium, 21 ounces; Small, 18 ounces; and Peewee, 15 ounces. Eggs are commercially graded AA, A, B, and C. Such marketing distinctions are made on the basis of appearance, rather than nutritive value—all grades being equally wholesome to eat. Grades AA and A are the ones you are most likely to find at your su-permarket, mainly for reasons of size and uniform attractiveness.

The color of their shell and yolk has nothing to do with the quality or nutritional value of eggs. Shell color is determined by the breed of hen producing the egg: breeds that lay brown eggs include Rhode Island Red, New Hampshire, and Plymouth Rock. In some locales, brown eggs are the preferred varieties, so accordingly their price is generally higher because of consumer demand.

STORAGE OF RAW AND COOKED EGGS

Unless you intend to use them immediately, always refrigerate eggs as soon as you get them home; their freshness and taste qualities deteriorate quite rapidly at normal room temperatures. To retain their freshness, it is better to store them in the cardboard or styrofoam commercial cartons they come in rather than in the molded plastic cups found in most refrigerator doors. Since eggs are porous and absorb odors easily, you should place the carton as far away from strong-smelling foods as possible.

While it is preferable for best results and taste to use them up within a week or two after purchase, properly stored raw eggs can keep in the refrigerator for as long as five weeks. Eggs with cracked or broken shells

should be used as soon as possible after purchase. Blemishes such as blood spots in yolk may be removed purely for appearance sake, but their presence in no way affects an egg's edibility.

Hard-cooked eggs refrigerated as soon as possible after cooking will keep well for up to one week. *Do not attempt to freeze hard-cooked eggs,* either in or out of their shells, since they become tough, watery, and unpalatable.

Uncooked frozen eggs will keep satisfactorily for up to nine months if carefully maintained in below-freezing conditions, according to the directions given below. When separated, raw egg whites can easily be frozen. Separate them into a freezer container, check that they are free of any spots of yolk, seal the container tightly, label it clearly with the number of egg whites and date, and then freeze. Or, for easier measuring later, you can freeze individual egg whites in the separate compartments of an ice cube tray and afterward transfer them to a regular freezer container for storage.

To freeze egg yolks or whole raw eggs, stir them very lightly with either ⅛ teaspoon salt,

1 ½ teaspoons sugar, or 1 ½ teaspoons of corn syrup per each ¼ cup of egg yolks (4 yolks) or whole eggs (2 unseparated eggs). Label the container with the date, number of eggs, and the ingredient added for storage purposes. (Sweetened frozen eggs will be used in preparing desserts.)

To thaw frozen egg whites, yolks, or whole eggs properly, move them from the freezer to the refrigerator compartment overnight. To beat eggs that have been frozen and thawed, for best results bring them to room temperature first.

SOME USES FOR EGG WHITES

Egg drops in soups; angel food, sponge, pound, and white cakes; meringues and white or boiled icings. Egg whites (and shells) are also used for clarifying consommé. One extra egg white added to a recipe will add volume to a soufflé.

SOME USES FOR EGG YOLKS

Aioli sauce, Hollandaise sauce, mayonnaise, salad dressing; custards and puddings;

yellow layer cake, pastry cream, and butter cream icings. Egg yolk acts as a thickener for cream sauces or gravy. For this purpose, it should be added just before serving; do not allow the sauce to boil after the yolk has been added.

COOKING METHODS

Though egg recipes are infinite in number, requiring only the imagination and instincts of the cook to continually create new and pleasing variations, there are six fundamental cooking methods and certain combinations of these on which the many culinary variations are based: soft-, medium-, and hard-cooked; poached; baked; fried. Descriptions of these basic techniques and various categories of egg dishes prepared with them will introduce the different general groupings of recipes, including some expert tips for best results in using them.

The Many Varieties of Eggs

Raw egg for "Prairie Oyster"

Soft-cooked egg

Medium-cooked eggs

Hard-cooked eggs

Poached egg

Baked eggs en cocotte

Fried egg

Scrambled eggs

Utensils and Serving Accessories for Eggs

A variety of ceramic egg cups and individual heat-proof casseroles for serving eggs.

◁

▷

Assorted glass and stainless steel kitchen utensils to be used in preparing eggs, such as wire egg slicers, separators, and shell removers.

Various types of pans used for frying eggs: steel, cast iron, and Teflon-coated. Also, an egg basket, a whisk, and a manual egg beater. ▷

◁ Different kinds of egg holders—glass, silver, ceramic— for table and for individual service, along with shears for clipping open eggshells.

Egg-Based Sauces

Aioli (Blender)

Yield: 1¾ cups

3 large garlic cloves, chopped
1½ Tb lemon juice (or wine vinegar)
½ tsp salt
3 egg yolks
1 cup olive oil

In the blender container, place garlic, lemon juice, salt, and egg yolks. Cover and blend on high speed until smooth.

Uncover and add the oil in a slow, steady stream; then blend on low speed. When sauce is so thick that oil becomes hard to incorporate, add 1 or 2 tablespoons of water, then add remaining oil. (Serve with fish or as a dip for fresh vegetables.)

Béarnaise

Yield: 2 cups

2 shallots, minced (or 4 scallions, without green tops)
1 Tb chopped fresh tarragon (or 1½ tsp dried)
½ tsp dried chervil (optional)
3 peppercorns, crushed
pinch of salt
⅓ cup tarragon wine vinegar
6 egg yolks
1 cup butter, melted

In a saucepan, combine shallots, 1 teaspoon of fresh tarragon (or ½ teaspoon dried), chervil, peppercorns, salt, and vinegar. Simmer over low heat until liquid has been reduced to 2 tablespoons. Cool to lukewarm.

Add egg yolks and beat until thick with a wire whisk or rotary beater. Place over low heat and gradually add butter. Beat until thickened and hot. Strain the sauce, stir in remaining 2 teaspoons of fresh tarragon (or 1 teaspoon dried) and serve hot. (Serve with poached eggs, steak, fried fish, or broiled chicken.)

Béchamel

Yield: 1 cup

2 Tb butter
½ tsp finely minced onion
2 Tb all-purpose flour
1 cup milk
salt and pepper
pinch of nutmeg, freshly grated

In a saucepan, melt butter over medium heat. Add onion and cook until transparent. Do not allow mixture to brown. Add flour and cook, stirring until well blended.

Meanwhile, bring milk almost to a boil. Pour into the flour mixture, stirring constantly, and cook until thick and smooth. Simmer another 5 minutes and season to taste with salt, pepper, and nutmeg.

This basic, medium-thick Béchamel is an all-purpose sauce called for in many of the recipes in this book. For thick Béchamel, called for in some soufflé recipes, follow the directions above, but use 3 tablespoons of butter and 3 tablespoons of flour.

Hollandaise

Yield: 1 cup

3 eggs yolks
1 Tb cold water
½ cup butter, melted
½ tsp salt
white pepper
1 Tb lemon juice
dash of cayenne pepper

Place egg yolks and cold water in the top of a double boiler. Set over an inch of hot (not boiling) water in the lower part, and beat with a wire whisk until fluffy. Add butter very slowly, whisking constantly, until thickened. Add salt, white pepper to taste, lemon juice, and cayenne. If you wish to thin the sauce, whisk in a tablespoon of hot water.

Mousseline

Fold 1 part whipped cream into 2 parts Hollandaise Sauce.

(Serve Hollandaise Sauce and Mousseline Sauce with eggs, fish, shellfish, and steamed broccoli, asparagus, or other cooked vegetables.)

Mayonnaise

Yield: 2 cups

3 egg yolks (at room temperature)
½ tsp salt
½ tsp dry mustard
dash of cayenne pepper
¾ cup olive oil
¾ cup vegetable oil
1 Tb lemon juice (or wine vinegar)

Beat egg yolks together with salt, mustard, and cayenne until thick and lemon-colored. Combine olive and vegetable oils, and add drop by drop to the yolk mixture, beating constantly. As mixture thickens, oil may be added a little faster. Stir in lemon juice and blend well, then chill.

Mayonnaise (Blender)

Yield: 1¼ cups

1 egg
½ tsp dry mustard
½ tsp salt
dash of cayenne pepper
2 Tb lemon juice (or wine vinegar)
½ cup olive oil
½ cup vegetable oil

In the blender container, place the egg, mustard, salt, cayenne, and lemon juice.

Combine olive and vegetable oils, and pour ¼ cup of oil mixture into blender. Cover and turn on to low speed. Uncover immediately and pour in remaining oil in a steady stream. Blend until smooth and thickened, then chill.

Swedish Egg Sauce

Yield: 1¼ cups

¼ cup butter
1 Tb all-purpose flour
1 cup milk
2 tsp prepared mustard
salt and pepper
2 hard-cooked eggs, chopped
2 tsp minced parsley

In a small saucepan, melt butter over medium heat. Add flour and cook, stirring until well blended. Gradually stir milk into flour mixture until well blended. Mix in mustard and salt and pepper to taste. Cook, stirring constantly, until thickened and bubbly. Gently blend in eggs and parsley. (Serve warm with baked or poached fish.)

Tartar Sauce

Yield: 2 cups

1 tsp prepared mustard
1½ cups mayonnaise
3 Tb minced scallions (including green tops)
1 Tb chopped sweet pickle
1 Tb chopped green olives
2 Tb capers

Combine mustard and mayonnaise and blend thoroughly. Add remaining ingredients and mix well, then chill. (Serve with fish or as a sandwich spread.)

Mayonnaise (pp. 13, 14)

Hollandaise and Mousseline (p. 13)

Egg Soups

Chicken Soup Pavia Style
(Zuppa Pavese)

Yield: 4 servings

4 cups rich chicken broth
butter
4 slices Italian bread
grated Parmesan cheese
4 eggs

In a saucepan, bring broth to a slow boil. Meanwhile, melt butter in a skillet, and sauté bread on both sides. Cut each slice into quarters and sprinkle with Parmesan cheese.

Break one egg at a time into a saucer, and slide it gently into the boiling broth. Turn heat low and simmer each egg 3 minutes, or until set. With a slotted spoon, remove eggs from broth and place each in a warm soup bowl.

Bring broth to a rolling boil, and pour through a strainer into soup bowls. Arrange bread slices around eggs, and sprinkle with a little more Parmesan.

Cornmeal Egg White Soup

Yield: 4 servings

1 Tb cornmeal
1 Tb grated Parmesan cheese
salt and pepper
pinch of nutmeg, freshly grated
3 egg whites
4 cups beef broth
croutons

In a small bowl, combine cornmeal, Parmesan, salt and pepper to taste, and nutmeg. In a large bowl, beat egg whites until stiff peaks form. Blend the dry mixture, a little at a time, into egg whites.

Bring broth to a boil, pour egg-white mixture in all at once, and stir vigorously with a wire whisk. Lower heat, cover, and simmer 5 minutes. Serve with croutons.

Egg and Cheese Dumpling Soup

Yield: 4 servings

1 cup grated Romano cheese
1 egg
2 tsp minced parsley
pinch of basil
salt and pepper
4 cups rich chicken broth

Combine cheese and egg with parsley, basil, and salt and pepper to taste. Blend thoroughly to make a stiff dough that can be formed into balls about 1 inch across. Add a little more cheese if necessary.

In a saucepan with a tight lid, bring broth to a steady simmer. Do not allow it to boil, or dumplings will fall apart when placed in the liquid. Spoon dumplings into broth gently, one at a time. Cover saucepan and turn heat off. Serve in about 10 minutes.

Egg Drop Soup

Yield: 4 servings

4 cups rich chicken broth
1 Tb cornstarch
2 Tb cold water
1 scallion, sliced thin (including green tops)
2 eggs
1 tsp dry sherry (optional)

In a medium-size saucepan, heat broth. Dissolve cornstarch in cold water, and add very gradually to simmering broth, stirring until it thickens slightly. Stir in chopped scallion, setting aside about 1 tablespoon of the green tops. Beat the eggs together with sherry. Gradually add egg mixture to broth, stirring constantly. As soon as it is all stirred in, remove from heat and serve garnished with the reserved scallion tops.

Egg Toast Broth

Yield: 4 servings

4 cups rich meat broth
4 egg yolks
2 tsp lemon juice
pinch of salt
12 small slices Italian (or French) bread, toasted
grated Parmesan cheese

Bring broth to a boil. Meanwhile, in a large saucepan, beat egg yolks until thick and lemon-colored. Add lemon juice and salt, then beat for another minute or so. Pour boiling broth over egg mixture, stirring constantly. Cook 5 minutes, stirring frequently; do not allow soup to boil, or the eggs will curdle. When slightly thickened, remove from heat.

To serve, pour over thin toasted bread slices in individual soup plates and sprinkle with Parmesan.

Greek Egg Soup
(Avgolemono)

Yield: 4 servings

4 cups rich chicken broth
4 heaping Tb cooked rice (optional)
4 eggs
juice of 1 lemon
pinch of salt

In a saucepan, bring broth to a boil. Add cooked rice. Beat the eggs with a wire whisk. Add lemon juice and salt to eggs. Whisking constantly, add half the broth to egg mixture. Pour egg and broth mixture back into saucepan. Turn heat low and cook, stirring frequently until eggs are set.

Mille-Fanti

Yield: 4 servings

4 cups chicken or beef broth
5 Tb bread crumbs
butter
2 eggs
pinch of nutmeg, freshly grated
salt and pepper
5 Tb grated Parmesan cheese

Bring broth to a boil. Meanwhile, sauté bread crumbs in a little butter. Beat eggs together with nutmeg and salt and pepper to taste. Blend in bread crumbs and Parmesan.

Pour mixture into boiling broth, stirring vigorously with a fork to keep eggs from curdling. As soon as broth returns to a gentle boil, pour into soup plates and serve sprinkled with a little additional cheese.

Onion Soup with Eggs

Yield: 4 servings

4 Tb butter
4 large onions, sliced
2 Tb all-purpose flour
6 cups rich beef broth, heated
4 egg yolks
4 heaping Tb grated Parmesan cheese
8 small slices French (or Italian) bread, toasted

In a large saucepan, melt butter and sauté onions over medium heat until golden brown. Stir in flour and blend well. Gradually pour in the broth, stirring with a wooden spoon until smooth. Cover and simmer for 30 minutes.

In a bowl, beat egg yolks lightly; blend in the Parmesan. Remove soup from heat, stir in egg mixture, and continue stirring until egg threads are set.

To serve, place 2 slices of toast in each of 4 soup plates and pour the soup over.

Roman Consommé with Egg Ribbons
(Stracciatella alla Romana)

Yield: 4 servings

4 cups chicken consommé
2 eggs
2 Tb grated Romano (or Parmesan) cheese
2 Tb minced parsley

In a saucepan, bring consommé to a slow boil. Meanwhile, beat eggs thoroughly and stir in the cheese and parsley. Slowly pour egg mixture into boiling consommé, stirring constantly with a fork until eggs set. Serve immediately.

Eggs in Gelatin (p. 32)

Rolled Crêpes in Broth

Yield: 4 servings

3 eggs
½ tsp salt
1 cup all-purpose flour
about ½ cup cold water
lard or butter
1 cup grated Parmesan cheese
cinnamon
4 or 5 cups rich chicken or beef broth, heated

With wire whisk, beat eggs and salt together thoroughly. Gradually add flour, beating constantly until smooth. Continue beating, and add enough cold water to make a batter about the consistency of thin cream. (This step can be done in a blender or food processor.)

Place an 8-inch crêpe pan or skillet over low heat. Grease the pan lightly with lard or butter. Pour in about 3 tablespoons of batter and tilt the pan immediately, so that batter completely coats the surface. Crêpes should be very thin. Cook until a delicate light brown, lift the crêpe, and flip it over to lightly brown the other side. Repeat with remaining batter, greasing the pan as necessary. Stack crêpes on a plate and keep warm.

To finish, sprinkle each crêpe with a tablespoon of Parmesan and a dash of cinnamon. Roll up loosely and place 2 crêpes side by side in each of 4 soup bowls. Place a second layer at right angles to the first. Pour in hot broth and serve.

Spanish Egg Soup

Yield: 4 servings

2 Tb butter
1 medium-size onion
1 garlic clove, minced
1 potato, peeled and chopped
1 stalk celery, chopped
2 Tb chopped parsley
½ tsp grated orange peel
salt and pepper
1 large tomato, peeled, seeded, and chopped
4 cups beef broth
4 eggs
4 slices buttered toast

In a large deep skillet, melt butter over medium heat. Sauté onion and garlic until golden. Stir in potato, celery, parsley, orange peel, and salt and pepper to taste. Sauté for 5 minutes, stirring occasionally. Stir in tomato and cook another 5 minutes. Add broth and simmer for 15 minutes.

Break one egg at a time into a saucer, then slide it very gently into simmering soup. Place a slice of buttered toast in each of 4 soup plates. With a slotted spoon, place a poached egg on each slice of toast, ladle soup over, and serve immediately.

Sauced Eggs and Other Dishes

Broccoli with Egg Sauce

Yield: 6 servings

about 1½ lb fresh broccoli (or 2 10-oz packages
*   frozen)*
2 eggs
1 Tb white wine vinegar
salt and pepper
2 Tb butter

Cook broccoli in lightly salted water until tender but still firm; drain and keep warm. Beat eggs together with vinegar, and season to taste with salt and pepper.

Melt butter in a small saucepan; remove temporarily from heat, to pour in the egg mixture, while stirring constantly. Place over heat again, still stirring constantly, just long enough to warm the sauce and thicken it slightly. (Do not allow it to boil.) Pour sauce over broccoli and serve hot.

Egg and Cheese Pie

Yield: 4 servings

4 slices bread (day-old)
8 eggs
salt and pepper
1 tsp dry mustard
dash of cayenne pepper
1 cup Muenster cheese, diced
2 Tb butter
minced parsley

Preheat broiler. Dice bread, and place in a bowl. Beat eggs together with salt and pepper to taste, mustard, and cayenne. Stir in cheese and blend well. Pour mixture over bread cubes, then stir briefly.

Melt butter in ovenproof skillet over medium heat. Pour in egg mixture, and cook just until bottom is set. Then, place under broiler until top is lightly browned. Turn out on a warm platter, garnish with parsley, and serve immediately.

Egg Fritters

Yield: 4 servings

1 Tb butter
2 medium-size fresh mushrooms, chopped
4 hard-cooked eggs, chopped fine
salt and pepper
1 cup thick Béchamel Sauce (see Index)
1½ cups all-purpose flour
2¼ tsp baking powder
1 egg white
2 egg yolks
⅔ cup milk
oil for deep frying

Melt butter in a small skillet, and sauté mushrooms. In a bowl, combine mushrooms, chopped eggs, salt and pepper to taste, and Béchamel Sauce. Place in refrigerator and chill for several hours. Shape mushroom-egg paste into small balls, about 1 inch in diameter. Place mushroom-egg balls in refrigerator while preparing the batter for frying.

Combine flour, baking powder, and ½ teaspoon of salt. Beat egg yolks, milk, and 2 tablespoons of oil together. Gradually add flour mixture to egg yolk mixture, beating constantly with a wire whisk. Fold egg white into batter.

In a deep fryer, heat oil to 375°. Dip chilled mushroom-egg balls in batter and fry, a few at a time so that temperature of cooking oil remains constant, until golden brown. Remove balls with a slotted spoon, and drain on paper towels.

"Eggs in Hell"

Yield: 4 servings

¼ cup olive oil
1 garlic clove, minced
1 medium-size onion, minced
2 cups tomato sauce
¼ tsp basil
¼ tsp thyme
1 Tb minced parsley
salt and pepper
8 eggs
8 small slices Italian bread
8 tsp grated Parmesan cheese

Heat oil in large skillet with a tight cover. Sauté garlic and onion until golden. Add tomato sauce, herbs, and salt and pepper to taste. Simmer sauce for 15 minutes, stirring occasionally. Break eggs into sauce, cover tightly, and cook over low heat for about 15 minutes, or until eggs are set.

Meanwhile, toast bread and put 2 slices on each of 4 plates. Place an egg and sauce on each slice of bread, and sprinkle with a teaspoon of grated Parmesan. Serve immediately.

Medium-Hard Eggs and Mushrooms on Toast (p. 29)

Baked Eggs with Italian Ham (p. 54)

Eggs Forester Style

Yield: 4 servings

8 hard-cooked eggs
½ cup olive oil
1 garlic clove, split
8 oz fresh mushrooms, sliced
16-oz can tomatoes
pinch of thyme
pinch of marjoram
salt and pepper
2 Tb minced parsley

Peel cooked eggs carefully, and slice in half lengthwise. Heat oil in a saucepan. Sauté garlic clove until golden brown and discard; then sauté mushrooms in seasoned oil. Add tomatoes, thyme, marjoram, and salt and pepper to taste. Stirring occasionally, cook for 20 minutes, or until sauce has thickened somewhat.

Preheat oven to 375°. Pour a layer of sauce into an ovenproof baking dish, and set out egg halves in it, cut side down. Sprinkle with parsley, and top with remaining sauce. Bake for 10 minutes.

Hunters' Eggs

Yield: 4 servings

4 Tb oil
1 medium-size onion, chopped fine
2 carrots, chopped fine
1 stalk celery, chopped fine
16-oz can tomatoes
¼ tsp sage
½ cup dry white wine
½ cup chicken or beef broth
salt and pepper
2 Tb minced parsley
8 hard-cooked eggs, sliced

Heat oil in a saucepan, and lightly sauté onion, carrots, and celery over medium heat. Add tomatoes and sage, then bring to a simmer. Lower the heat, cover saucepan, and gently simmer for 20 minutes. Add wine, broth, and salt and pepper to taste. Cook, uncovered, for another 10 minutes, or until sauce thickens somewhat.

Pour sauce into large shallow casserole, and stir in parsley, reserving a little for garnish. Place over medium heat and bring to a boil. Lower the heat; then arrange egg slices in casserole, taking care not to break them. Heat just long enough to warm eggs, garnish with reserved parsley, and serve hot.

Mexican Eggs

Yield: 4 servings

1 large green pepper
1 small chili pepper (or ¼ tsp red pepper flakes)
2 medium-size tomatoes
1 garlic clove
4 Tb oil
1 cup chicken or beef broth
salt and pepper
4 slices bacon
4 eggs
2 Tb butter
4 slices toast

Clean and seed the green pepper, chili pepper, and tomatoes. Chop coarse, then put in a blender or food processor. Peel and slice garlic, add to vegetables in container, and blend to coarse purée. Pour mix into a saucepan, add oil and broth, season with salt and pepper to taste, and cook over low heat, stirring occasionally, until the sauce becomes quite thick.

Fry bacon until crisp, and drain on a paper towel. Fry eggs in butter. Arrange toast on a warm platter, place a strip of fried bacon on each slice, top with a fried egg, and spoon sauce over the eggs. Serve immediately.

Marie's Peppers and Eggs

Yield: 4 servings

2 lb Italian frying peppers
3 Tb oil
8-oz can tomatoes
salt and pepper
pinch of oregano
4 eggs

Wipe peppers with a damp cloth, cut open lengthwise, and remove core and seeds. Slice peppers in strips.

Place oil in large skillet, add sliced peppers, and set skillet over low heat. Sauté peppers until they become slightly limp, while stirring constantly. Add tomatoes, salt and pepper to taste, and a generous pinch of oregano. Crush tomatoes slightly with the edge of a wooden spoon. Stir gently to blend, cover the skillet, and cook until tender. Beat eggs and stir them into the pan, blending thoroughly. Cover pan and turn off heat. Let stand about 5 minutes, or until eggs are firm.

Piperade

Yield: 4 servings

3 Tb oil
2 medium-size onions, sliced
4 Italian frying peppers, cut in strips
2 medium-size tomatoes, chopped
2 Tb minced parsley
salt and pepper
6 eggs

Heat oil in heavy covered skillet. Sauté onions until golden. (Do not let them brown.) Add peppers and cook until soft. Add tomatoes and parsley, seasoning to taste with salt and pepper. Cover skillet and cook until vegetables are very soft

Beat eggs together with salt and pepper to taste, and pour into vegetable mixture. Stir constantly and gently with wooden spoon until eggs are cooked through, but still moist and creamy in consistency.

San Francisco Eggs and Hamburger

Yield: 4 servings

1 lb fresh spinach (or 10-oz
    package frozen chopped)
1 lb lean ground beef
1 garlic clove, minced
1 large onion, chopped fine
salt and pepper
pinch of oregano
pinch of basil
6 eggs
½ cup grated Parmesan cheese
8 slices sourdough bread

Wash spinach thoroughly, cook in lightly salted water, and drain well. Chop coarse.

In a heavy skillet, brown meat over medium heat, and drain off excess fat. Add garlic, onion, salt and pepper to taste, oregano, and basil. Stir in chopped spinach. Beat eggs lightly together with grated Parmesan; add to contents of skillet and cook, stirring gently, until eggs are set. Serve along with toasted sourdough bread.

Scotch Eggs

Yield: 4 servings

*1 lb bulk sausage meat (or equal amount of
    stuffing from any regular commercial sausages)*
4 hard-cooked eggs
all-purpose flour
1 egg, beaten lightly
fine dry bread crumbs
oil for deep frying

Divide meat into 4 patties. Peel eggs, then enclose each one in sausage meat. Dredge in flour. dip in beaten egg, and roll in bread crumbs.

In a deep fryer, heat oil to 375°. Fry breaded eggs, one at a time so that temperature of cooking oil remains constant, until sausage meat is well browned. Remove with a slotted spoon, and drain on paper towels.

Strata

Yield: 4 to 6 servings

softened butter
6 slices bread (day-old)
1 cup cheddar cheese, shredded
6 eggs
1½ cups milk
1 tsp dry mustard
salt
dash of cayenne

Butter bread slices, then cut in 1-inch cubes. In a buttered 8-cup casserole, arrange alternate layers of bread cubes and shredded cheese.

Beat eggs lightly. Then beat in milk, mustard, salt to taste, and cayenne. Pour gently over bread and cheese. Allow to stand, covered, for at least 1 hour. (Strata may also be refrigerated, covered, for several hours or even overnight before baking.) Preheat oven to 350°. Bake uncovered for about 1 hour, or until golden brown.

French Toast

Yield: 4 servings

4 eggs
3 Tb milk
dash of salt
dash of nutmeg (or cinnamon), freshly grated
8 slices bread (day-old)
4 Tb butter

In a shallow dish, beat together eggs, milk, salt, and nutmeg or cinnamon. Soak 4 slices of bread in egg mixture, one at a time, about a minute for each side. Melt half the butter in large skillet over high heat. (Do not let it brown.) Place egg-soaked bread in skillet, lower heat, and brown both sides lightly. Repeat procedure with other 4 slices. Sprinkle egg toast with powdered sugar, or else serve with pancake syrup or jam.

Zucchini Veneto Style

Yield: 4 servings

8 small zucchini squash
1 Tb butter
salt
2 eggs
½ cup milk
6 Tb grated Parmesan cheese
pinch of mint (or basil), preferably fresh

Rinse zucchini, and boil them in lightly salted water for about 10 minutes. Dry, trim, and cut zucchini into julienne strips. Melt butter in heatproof casserole, and add the squash. Season with salt, cover the casserole, and cook for a few minutes over low heat.

Beat eggs together with milk, then add grated Parmesan and mint (or basil) and blend well. Pour egg mixture over zucchini, and cook for another few minutes, just until eggs are set. Serve at once.

Stuffed Tomatoes (p. 34)

Soft-, Medium-, and Hard-Cooked Eggs

EGGS COOKED IN THE SHELL

For best results when cooking eggs in the shell, use 2- or 3-day-old eggs and first bring the eggs to room temperature. Place them in a saucepan, and cover with cool water to a depth of at least 1 inch above the eggs. Place the saucepan over high heat, and bring the water quickly to a boil. Immediately reduce the heat, then cook the eggs at a very slow simmer. They should not be *boiled*. Time the cooking from the moment that simmering begins.

For soft-cooked eggs, simmer for 1 to 3 minutes. They will be cooked, but still runny.

For medium-cooked eggs (or eggs mollet), simmer for 4 to 5 minutes. The whites will be firm, while the yolks remain soft.

For hard-cooked eggs, simmer for 7 to 10 minutes. The whites will be firm, and the yolks solid but creamy.

When cooked eggs are done to the desired degree, plunge them immediately in cold water. This will stop further cooking and prevent any greenish-gray coloring on the surface of yolks.

Should the question arise, you can tell a cooked egg from a raw one by spinning the egg on its side: a cooked egg will spin; a raw egg will wobble.

Soft-Cooked Eggs with Toast Fingers

Yield: 4 servings

6 slices firm-textured white bread
oil
milk
all-purpose flour
8 eggs
about 2 Tb butter, softened
salt and pepper

Trim the crusts and cut bread into strips about ½ inch thick. Pour enough oil into a skillet to come about ½ inch up the sides of the pan. Place over medium-high heat until the oil becomes quite hot, but not smoking. Dip the bread in milk, dust lightly with flour, and fry on both sides until golden brown. Drain on paper towels.

Place eggs in a saucepan and add cold water to cover completely. Bring to a boil over high heat, turn heat low, and simmer gently for 3 to 4 minutes. Remove eggs from hot water immediately. Using a spoon to shell and scoop them out, put 2 cooked eggs in each serving dish. Dot with a little softened butter, and sprinkle with salt and pepper to taste. Surround the soft-cooked eggs with toast fingers and serve immediately.

Medium-Hard Eggs with Bacon

Yield: 4 servings

8 eggs
8 slices bacon, fairly thick
3 Tb oil
8 slices bread

Place eggs in a saucepan, and add cold water to cover completely. Bring to a boil over high heat, turn heat low, and simmer eggs gently for exactly 5 minutes. Plunge eggs into cold water, then peel carefully and keep warm.

Fry bacon and drain on paper towels. Heat oil in a large skillet, and fry bread slices golden brown on both sides. Arrange browned bread slices on a serving platter, set a cooked egg on each, garnish with bacon, and serve.

Medium-Hard Eggs and Mushrooms on Toast

Yield: 4 servings

8 oz fresh mushrooms
2 Tb butter
salt
4 thick slices bacon, diced
1 cup tomato sauce
8 eggs
oil
8 slices firm-textured white bread

Clean and slice mushrooms. Melt butter in a medium-size skillet, and sauté the mushrooms. Add salt to taste. In another skillet, sauté bacon until crisp and brown. Drain on paper towels.

Bring tomato sauce to a boil, turn heat low, and simmer briefly to thicken. Place eggs in a saucepan, and add cold water to cover completely. Bring to a boil over high heat, turn heat low, and simmer eggs gently for 4 to 5 minutes. Do not overcook. Plunge eggs into cold water, then peel carefully and keep them warm.

Heat just enough oil to grease very lightly a large skillet. Add bread slices and brown them on both sides. Remove bread to a warm platter and cover each slice with mushrooms. Sprinkle with diced bacon, place an egg in the center of each, and spoon tomato sauce over each egg.

Baked Eggs and Asparagus

Yield: 4 servings

1 lb fresh asparagus, cleaned and trimmed
  (or 10-oz package frozen)
2 cups Béchamel Sauce (see Index)
½ cup grated Parmesan cheese
6 hard-cooked eggs, sliced
½ cup bread crumbs
2 Tb butter

Cook asparagus, drain well, and chop. Heat Béchamel Sauce, add grated Parmesan, and blend well. Gently stir asparagus into the sauce and remove from heat.

Preheat oven to 350°. Generously butter a baking dish. Line the dish with a layer of sliced eggs, and gradually pour a thin layer of sauce over the eggs. Add another layer of egg slices, then sauce, and continue layering with sauce and eggs, finishing with a layer of sauce. Sprinkle with bread crumbs, dot with butter, and bake a few minutes, or just until heated through.

Creamed Eggs in Patty Shells

Yield: 6 servings

1 package frozen patty shells (6)
1 Tb butter
1 medium-size onion, sliced thin
1½ cups Béchamel Sauce (see Index)
pinch of dry mustard
salt and pepper
9 hard-cooked eggs, sliced
minced parsley

Bake patty shells according to directions on the package. In a heavy saucepan, melt butter and sauté onion until tender. Add Béchamel Sauce, mustard, and salt and pepper to taste. Blend thoroughly and cook for 5 minutes, stirring occasionally.

Add eggs, then cook another minute. Do not allow sauce to boil. Pour into patty shells and garnish with parsley.

Curried Eggs

Yield: 4 servings

2 Tb butter
1 medium-size onion, sliced thin
2 tsp curry powder
dash of allspice
¼ tsp powdered ginger
dash of cayenne pepper
2 cups Béchamel Sauce (see Index)
¼ cup unsweetened applesauce
salt and pepper
4 slices bread
8 hard-cooked eggs, sliced

In a heavy saucepan, melt butter and sauté onion until transparent. Add curry powder and cook, stirring with a wooden spoon, until onion is tender. Blend in allspice, ginger, and cayenne. Combine Béchamel and applesauce, and add salt and pepper to taste. Stir into onion mix, then cook for 5 minutes, stirring occasionally.

Toast the bread, butter it, and cut diagonally into triangles. Add eggs to sauce, and cook 1 minute. Do not allow sauce to boil.

To serve, pour curried eggs into a deep serving dish and surround with triangles of buttered toast.

Mozzarella Omelet (p. 37)

Eggs in Gelatin

Yield: 4 servings

5 hard-cooked eggs
2 cups cooked chicken, cut in strips
1 cup ham, cut in strips
1 cup mayonnaise
2 envelopes unflavored gelatin
3½ cups chicken consommé

Peel, slice, and reserve 4 eggs. Peel and chop the remaining egg; place it in a mixing bowl with chicken, ham, and mayonnaise. Blend gently but thoroughly.

Soak gelatin in ¼ cup of cold consommé. Heat remaining consommé, add gelatin mixture, and stir until dissolved. Choose a tall 8-cup mold with straight sides, and rinse it in cold water (or spray very lightly with vegetable oil). Fill the mold with gelatin to a depth of about 2 inches, then tilt and turn the mold so that its sides are thoroughly coated with gelatin. Place in refrigerator until set.

In the bottom of the mold, place 4 or 5 egg slices in a circle. Carefully pour in enough gelatin to make a thin layer over the eggs, then place in refrigerator until set. Next, spoon in a third of the chicken and ham mixture, leaving a little space around the sides. Top with another circle of egg slices, and pour in enough gelatin to cover, carefully filling the space around the sides. Place in refrigerator until set. Continue layering and chilling to set. Finish with a layer of gelatin and chill until set. Unmold on a platter when ready to serve. The mold may be garnished with additional sliced eggs, vegetables, or salad greens such as parsley, watercress, or lettuce leaves.

Hard-Cooked Eggs with Green Mayonnaise

Yield: 4 servings

3 Tb minced parsley
2 Tb minced chives (or scallion tops)
¾ cup mayonnaise
1 or 2 Tb lemon juice
½ tsp Dijon mustard
4 hard-cooked eggs
sprigs of parsley (or watercress)

In a bowl, combine thoroughly the parsley, chives, mayonnaise, lemon juice, and mustard. (You may use a blender for this step.) Peel eggs, cut them in half lengthwise, and place on a serving dish, with the cut side down. Coat eggs with green mayonnaise, and garnish with sprigs of parsley or watercress.

Hard-Cooked Eggs in Tuna Sauce

Yield: 4 servings

1 large scallion (including green tops)
2 Tb oil
16-oz can tomatoes
salt
½ tsp basil
6½-oz can chunk tuna
8 eggs

Preheat oven to 350°. Mince the scallion. Heat oil in a saucepan, and sauté the scallion briefly. Put tomatoes through a food mill or purée in a blender, and add to the scallion. Season with salt to taste and basil. Simmer until sauce is somewhat reduced.

Drain tuna, then pound in a mortar or chop very fine, and stir into sauce. Peel eggs, and cut in quarters, lengthwise. Arrange eggs in a sunburst pattern in a heatproof serving dish, cover with sauce, and bake for 10 minutes.

Lemon Stuffed Eggs

Yield: 4 to 6 servings

6 hard-cooked eggs
2 Tb olive oil
2 Tb lemon juice
salt
dash of cayenne pepper
12 anchovy fillets

Peel eggs, and cut in half lengthwise. Scoop yolks into a small bowl. Add olive oil, lemon juice, salt to taste, and cayenne. With a fork, mash to a creamy consistency, and fill egg whites with the mixture.

Cut each anchovy fillet in half lengthwise, and arrange in a crisscross pattern over the filled eggs. Chill slightly before serving.

Mustard Deviled Eggs

Yield: 4 to 6 servings

6 hard-cooked eggs
3 Tb mayonnaise
1 Tb chopped parsley
1 Tb chopped chives
½ tsp Dijon mustard
salt and pepper
12 thin strips pimento
6 black olives, sliced

Peel eggs and cut in half lengthwise. Scoop yolks into a small bowl. Add mayonnaise, parsley, chives, and mustard. With a fork, mash mix to a creamy consistency. Season with salt and pepper to taste, and fill egg whites with the mixture. Garnish each egg with a pimento strip and black olive slices.

Stuffed Eggs with Mushrooms and Tuna

Yield: 4 servings

6 hard-cooked eggs
3½-oz can tuna in oil
2 Tb oil
1 cup sliced fresh mushrooms
2 Tb dry vermouth
salt and pepper
2 Tb butter
2 Tb all-purpose flour
2 cups milk
1 tsp paprika
1 heaping Tb grated Parmesan cheese

Peel and slice eggs lengthwise. Scoop out yolks, and combine them with tuna in a blender or food processor. Blend to a coarse purée. Spoon mixture generously into egg whites.

Heat oil in a skillet over medium-high heat, and sauté mushrooms for about 10 minutes, stirring occasionally. Stir in vermouth and cook until it evaporates. Season to taste with salt and pepper.

Melt butter in a saucepan, add flour and cook, stirring until well blended. Gradually add milk and cook, stirring occasionally, until sauce is smooth and slightly thickened. Season with paprika and salt and pepper to taste, then blend in Parmesan.

Preheat oven to 350°. Arrange filled eggs in a greased baking dish, top with sautéed mushrooms, and pour sauce over all. Bake for 20 minutes.

Stuffed Tomatoes

Yield: 4 servings

4 hard-cooked eggs
1 Tb minced parsley
4 large tomatoes
salt
6½-oz can chunk tuna
3½ Tb butter, softened
4 or 5 Tb mayonnaise
juice of 1 small lemon
8 black olives

Peel eggs, slice them in half lengthwise, and separate yolks from whites. Chop yolks and whites separately, adding parsley to yolks.

Cut tomatoes in half horizontally, and scoop out seeds and pulp. Salt tomato shells lightly, and invert them to drain. Next, drain tunafish and place in a bowl. With a fork, flake the fish, then add butter, mayonnaise, and lemon juice and mix well.

Fill tomato shells with tuna mixture. Cover half the shell with egg yolk and parsley mixture, and top the other half with chopped egg white. Garnish with olives and serve.

Asparagus and Mushroom Frittata (p. 40)

Tomato and Mozzarella Frittata (p. 45)

Omelets and Frittatas

OMELETS

A good omelet starts with a good omelet pan. It should be fairly heavy, of iron or cast aluminum, and with rounded curving sides and a long handle. Ideally, the pan should be used only for omelets, because multipurpose skillets develop rough surfaces that will cause eggs to stick. An omelet pan is not to be washed, but instead should be wiped clean with paper towels immediately after use. If there has been any sticking, heat the pan, sprinkle it with salt, and then rub it with the paper towels.

Use the freshest eggs you can get, and beat them briefly with a fork or wire whisk. The eggs should be lightly beaten, not frothy.

Small, 2- or 3-egg omelets can be cooked in seconds over high heat, then kept in a warm oven for a few minutes until serving time. A fluffy (or puffy, or American-style) omelet should be served immediately.

A classic French-style rolled omelet requires some practice. Most of the following recipes—either basic or filled—simply call for folding the omelet, which is an easy, no-fuss technique.

Fluffy Omelet

Yield: 4 servings

6 eggs, separated
½ tsp salt
⅓ cup water
pepper
2 Tb butter

Preheat oven to 325°. Place egg whites in a large bowl, add salt and water, and beat until stiff moist peaks form. To egg yolks, add pepper to taste and beat until thick and lemon-colored. Fold gently into egg whites.

Melt butter in a medium-size ovenproof skillet over medium-high heat. Pour in egg mix, lower heat, and cook about 5 minutes, until omelet is puffy and the bottom is lightly browned. Then, place skillet in oven and bake for 12 to 15 minutes, or just until a knife inserted in the center comes out clean. Serve immediately.

Fresh Tomato Omelet

Yield: 4 servings

4 large ripe tomatoes
1½ Tb minced fresh basil (or ½ tsp dried)
5 eggs
salt and pepper
2 Tb butter

Place tomatoes briefly in boiling water, then peel them. Cut them in half, remove seeds, and chop the pulp coarse. Toss with 1 tablespoon of minced basil and set aside.

Beat eggs together with salt and pepper to taste. Melt butter over medium-high heat. (Do not let butter turn brown.) Pour in the eggs. As eggs begin to set, lower heat. Lift edges of the omelet with fork to allow uncooked portion to flow underneath. Tilt pan and shake it vigorously, so bottom does not stick.

When eggs have set, spoon tomatoes over half the omelet, fold the other half over, and cook just long enough to warm tomatoes. Turn out on a warm platter, sprinkle with remaining basil, and serve immediately.

Ham Omelet

Yield: 4 servings

4 oz cooked ham, sliced
3 Tb butter
6 eggs
dash of salt
2 Tb minced parsley

Chop ham slices and sauté in 1 tablespoon of butter. Beat eggs together with salt, then stir in parsley and sautéed ham.

Melt remaining 2 tablespoons of butter in large omelet pan over medium-high heat. As soon as butter stops foaming in the pan, pour in egg mix. As eggs begin to set, lower heat. Lift edges of the omelet with fork or thin spatula to allow uncooked portion to flow underneath. Tilt pan and shake it vigorously, so bottom does not stick.

Slip a broad spatula under the eggs when set, fold over, and turn out on a warm platter.

Mozzarella Omelet

Yield: 4 servings

6 eggs
salt and pepper
⅓ cup grated Parmesan cheese
⅔ cup mozzarella cheese, shredded
2 Tb butter

In a bowl, beat eggs together with salt and pepper to taste. Stir in grated Parmesan, and blend well.

Melt butter in a large omelet pan over medium-high heat. (Do not let butter turn brown.) As soon as butter stops foaming, pour in egg mix. As soon as eggs begin to set, lower heat, and lift edges of the omelet with fork to allow uncooked portion to flow underneath. Tilt pan and shake it vigorously, so bottom does not stick. Sprinkle mozzarella over half the omelet, fold the other half over, and cook just until cheese melts. Slip a broad spatula under eggs when set and turn out on a warm platter.

Omelet with Croutons

Yield: 4 servings

3 Tb butter
2 cups plain or seasoned croutons
6 eggs
salt and pepper
1 Tb minced parsley
4 heaping Tb grated Parmesan cheese

Heat 2 Tb of butter in skillet, and sauté croutons until lightly browned. Set aside. Beat eggs together with salt and pepper to taste, and add parsley.

Heat remaining tablespoon of butter in a large omelet pan over medium-high heat. Blend croutons quickly into eggs. As soon as butter stops foaming in the pan, pour in egg mix. As eggs begin to set, lower heat. Lift edges of the omelet with fork or thin spatula to allow uncooked portion to flow underneath. Tilt pan and shake it vigorously, so bottom does not stick. Slip a broad spatula under eggs when set, fold over, and. turn out on a warm platter.

Saffron Omelet

Yield: 4 servings

6 eggs
salt
2 Tb minced onion
2 Tb butter
pinch of saffron
1 cup tomato sauce (preferably homemade), heated

In a bowl, beat eggs together with a pinch of salt. Sauté onion in 1 tablespoon of butter with saffron. Season lightly with salt. Cool and blend into eggs.

Melt remaining butter in omelet pan over medium-high heat. (Do not let butter turn brown.) As soon as butter stops foaming, pour in egg mix. As eggs begin to set, lower heat. Lift edges of the omelet with fork to allow uncooked portion to flow underneath. Tilt pan and shake it vigorously, so bottom does not stick.

For a classic rolled omelet, slide eggs toward one side of the pan, rolling omelet carefully with fork. For a simple folded omelet, slip a broad spatula under eggs when set, fold over, and turn out on a warm platter. Serve with the warmed tomato sauce.

Chinese Frittata (p. 41)

FRITTATAS

The *frittata*, an Italian version of the omelet, is one of the most versatile of egg dishes. It may be a savory main course for luncheon or dinner, can be be served hot or cold, and makes excellent picnic fare. Practically anything can go into the preparation of a frittata: meat, poultry, seafood, vegetables, cheese, rice, or noodles. The combinations and variations possible with this tasty egg dish are virtually limitless.

The traditional way to cook a frittata is to brown it on one side like a pancake, invert it on a plate, and then slide it back into the skillet to brown the other side. Because it is all-important that none of the egg sticks to the pan, use an omelet pan or other skillet which is used *only* for making frittatas and omelets.

Some cooks find it easier to brown the underside of the eggs in an ovenproof skillet and then put it under the broiler briefly to finish cooking. A third method is probably easiest of all: Brown the eggs on one side, cover the skillet and remove from the heat, and let the frittata stand until the top is set. Whatever the method followed, the end result may either be cooked through or be slightly creamy in the center, according to individual taste. The frittata should be served cut in pie wedges.

Asparagus and Mushroom Frittata

Yield: 4 servings

6 oz fresh mushrooms
1 lb fresh asparagus (or 10-oz package frozen)
2 Tb butter
4 Tb oil
salt and pepper
2 slices cooked ham, cut in strips
6 eggs
⅓ cup grated Parmesan cheese

Clean mushrooms and cut into thin slices. Cook asparagus until tender but crisp. Drain and chop into bite-size pieces. In a saucepan, melt butter with 2 tablespoons of oil, and sauté mushrooms for 5 minutes. Season to taste with salt and pepper, add ham, and stir gently. Cook until mushrooms are done, drain, and reserve.

Beat eggs, and season with salt and pepper. Stir in mushroom mixture, asparagus, and grated Parmesan. Blend well. In a heavy skillet, heat remaining oil over medium heat. Pour the egg mixture into pan, and blend gently with wooden spoon. Turn heat to medium-low. Cook the frittata until golden brown and top is well set. Invert frittata on a plate and slide it back into skillet, with uncooked side down. Cook until that side is golden brown. Slide the frittata onto a warm platter and serve immediately.

Chinese Frittata

Yield: 4 servings

½ lb lean pork
1 Tb soy sauce
4 Tb oil
6 eggs
pinch of salt

Cut pork in very thin strips, mix with soy sauce, and marinate for 30 minutes. In a heavy skillet, heat oil and brown pork strips over medium heat.

Beat eggs together with salt, and pour mix over pork in the skillet. Stir gently with a wooden spoon, and turn heat to medium-low. Cook the frittata until bottom is golden brown and top is well set. Invert frittata on a plate and slide it back into skillet, with uncooked side down. Cook until that side is golden brown. Slide the frittata onto a warm platter and serve immediately.

Ham and Tomato Frittata

Yield: 4 servings

4 Tb oil
2 garlic cloves, crushed
½ cup cooked ham, chopped
½ cup chopped tomatoes, drained
6 eggs
salt and pepper
1 Tb fresh chopped basil (or ¼ tsp dried)
½ cup grated Parmesan cheese

In a saucepan, heat 2 tablespoons of oil, and cook garlic until golden in color. Add ham and sauté briefly. Add chopped tomatoes, bring to a boil, turn heat low, and simmer for 6 or 7 minutes. Remove from heat.

In a large bowl, beat eggs together with salt and pepper to taste. Stir in tomato sauce, basil, and grated Parmesan and blend well. In a heavy skillet, heat 2 remaining tablespoons of oil over medium-high heat. Pour in the egg mixture, and blend gently with wooden spoon. Turn heat to medium-low. Cook the frittata until bottom is golden brown and top is well set. Invert frittata on a plate and slide it back into skillet, with uncooked side down. Cook until that side is golden brown. Slide the frittata onto a warm platter and serve immediately.

Hearty Scallion Frittata

Yield: 4 servings

3 bunches large scallions
all-purpose flour
3 Tb oil
6 eggs
salt and pepper
½ cup grated pecorino (or Romano) cheese

Clean and trim scallions. Cut off bulbs, and reserve stalk and green tops for other use. Dust scallion bulbs lightly with flour. In a heavy skillet, heat oil and sauté scallions over medium heat until golden brown.

Beat eggs, then add salt and pepper to taste and grated cheese, blending well. Pour mixture over scallions in skillet, and stir gently with wooden spoon. Turn heat to medium-low. Cook the frittata until bottom is golden brown and top is well set. Invert frittata on a plate and slide it back into skillet, with uncooked side down. Cook until that side is golden brown. Slide the frittata onto a warm platter and serve immediately.

Noodle and Sausage Frittata

Yield: 4 servings

2 cups cold cooked noodles
8 eggs
4 heaping Tb grated Parmesan cheese
½ lb bulk pork sausage (or equivalent amount of
   stuffing from commercial sausages)
3 Tb oil
4 slices semisoft cheese (e.g., Bel Paese, Muenster)

Chop noodles (they can be sauced left-overs) into bite-size pieces. Beat eggs lightly, then stir in Parmesan and noodles and blend well. Crumble sausage meat into skillet, and sauté until well browned.

In a large heavy skillet, heat oil over medium-high heat. Pour in half the noodle mixture, and blend gently with wooden spoon. Arrange slices of cheese over noodles and eggs, and top with cooked sausage. Cover with remaining noodle mixture. Turn heat to medium-low. Cook the frittata until bottom is golden brown and top is well set. Invert frittata on a plate and slide it back into skillet, with uncooked side down. Cook until that side is golden brown. Slide the frittata onto a warm platter and serve immediately.

Pepper and Onion Frittata

Yield: 4 servings

¼ cup oil
1 medium-size onion, sliced thin
3 large bell peppers, seeded and cut in strips
8 eggs
salt and pepper
pinch of oregano

In a skillet, heat oil over medium heat. Sauté onion just until transparent, add peppers, and sauté until vegetables are tender. Beat eggs; season to taste with salt and pepper and oregano. Pour egg mix into skillet, and blend gently with wooden spoon. Turn heat to medium-low. Cook the frittata until bottom is golden brown and top is well set. Invert frittata on a plate and slide it back into skillet, with uncooked side down. Cook until that side is golden brown. Slide the frittata onto a warm platter and serve immediately.

Rice Frittata

Yield: 4 servings

8 eggs
salt and pepper
½ tsp thyme
1 Tb minced parsley
½ cup cooked rice
1 Tb oil

Beat eggs lightly together with salt and pepper to taste, thyme, and parsley. Blend in cooked rice.

Heat oil in skillet over medium-high heat. Pour in egg mixture, and stir gently with wooden spoon. Turn heat to medium-low. Cook the frittata until bottom is golden brown and top is well set. Invert frittata on a plate and slide it back into skillet, with uncooked side down. Cook until that side is golden brown. Slide the frittata onto a warm platter and serve immediately.

Ham and Tomato Frittata (p. 41)

Savory Chicken Frittata

Yield: 4 servings

1 medium-size onion, chopped
3 Tb oil
2 small stalks celery, chopped
dash of sage
dash of thyme
1 cup cooked chicken, chopped
2 Tb chopped parsley
6 eggs
salt and pepper

In a large heavy skillet, sauté onion in 1 tablespoon of oil. Add celery, and cook until vegetables are tender. Stir in sage and thyme, cook briefly, then add chicken and continue cooking until heated through. Stir in parsley.

In a bowl, lightly beat eggs together with salt and pepper to taste. Stir in chicken mixture, and blend thoroughly. Heat 2 remaining tablespoons of oil in large heavy skillet over medium-high heat. Pour in egg mixture, stirring gently with wooden spoon, and then turn heat to medium-low. Cook the frittata until bottom is golden brown and top is well set. Invert frittata on a plate and slide it back into skillet, with uncooked side down. Cook until that side is golden brown. Slide the frittata onto a warm platter and serve immediately.

Spinach Frittata

Yield: 4 servings

1 lb tender young spinach (or other leafy greens)
4 tsp butter
2 heaping Tb grated Parmesan cheese
pinch of nutmeg
1/4 tsp grated lemon peel
6 eggs
salt and pepper
1/4 cup oil

Rinse spinach in several changes of water to remove all traces of sand. Cook greens in a little boiling salted water. Squeeze dry and chop coarse. In a saucepan, heat half the butter, and sauté chopped spinach lightly over low heat for about 10 minutes. Add grated Parmesan, nutmeg, and the lemon rind. Remove from heat and mix well.

Beat eggs together with salt and pepper to taste, and pour into spinach mixture. In a skillet, heat oil and 2 remaining teaspoons of butter over medium-high heat. Pour in egg-spinach mixture; blend gently with wooden spoon. Turn heat to medium-low. Cook the frittata until bottom is golden brown and top is well set. Invert frittata on a plate and slide it back into skillet, with uncooked side down. Cook until that side is golden brown. Slide the frittata onto a warm platter and serve immediately.

Tomato and Mozzarella Frittata

Yield: 4 servings

6 eggs
salt
4 Tb oil
½ cup chopped tomato, drained
4 oz mozzarella cheese, shredded

In a large bowl, beat eggs along with a little salt. In a saucepan, heat 2 tablespoons of oil, add chopped tomato, and cook over medium heat for a few minutes. Cool the sauce, and blend into eggs.

In a heavy skillet, heat 2 remaining tablespoons of oil over medium-high heat. Pour in egg mixture, and mix well with a fork. Turn heat to medium-low. Cook the frittata until bottom is golden brown and top is well set. Invert frittata on plate and slide it back into skillet, with uncooked side down. Sprinkle chopped mozzarella evenly over the top. Cook until cheese has melted and the frittata is golden brown on the bottom. Slide the frittata onto a warm platter and serve immediately.

Tuna Frittata

Yield: 4 servings

7-oz can chunk tuna
6 eggs
salt and pepper
½ tsp oregano
1 Tb minced parsley
1 garlic clove, minced
3 anchovy fillets, minced
2 Tb oil

Drain and flake the tuna. In a bowl, beat eggs lightly. Add salt and pepper to taste, together with oregano, parsley, garlic, anchovies, and tuna.

Heat oil in a large, heavy skillet over medium-high heat. Pour in egg mixture, and turn heat to medium-low. Cook the frittata until bottom is golden brown and top is well set. Invert frittata on a plate and slide it back into skillet, with uncooked side down. Cook until that side is golden brown. Slide the frittata onto a warm platter and serve immediately.

Fried and Scrambled Eggs

Fried Eggs Neapolitan

Yield: 4 servings

4 Tb oil
4 slices mozzarella cheese
8 eggs
salt
oregano
8 anchovy fillets
⅔ cup tomato sauce (preferably homemade)

In each of 4 small-size cook-and-serve skillets, heat 1 tablespoon of oil over low heat. Place a single slice of cheese in each skillet, and break 2 eggs over each slice of cheese. Put a pinch of salt and oregano on each egg, and top with an anchovy fillet. Pour a generous tablespoon of tomato sauce over each egg, then fry until the white is set.

Fried Eggs and Hash

Yield: 4 servings

2 Tb oil
2 medium-size onions, chopped
2 cups cooked beef (or pork), diced
2 cups firm cooked potatoes, diced
salt and pepper
1 Tb butter
4 eggs
1 Tb chopped parsley

In a large skillet, heat oil and sauté onions until golden. With a wooden spoon, blend in meat, potatoes, and salt and pepper to taste. Cook until the potatoes are lightly browned.

In a medium-size skillet, melt butter over medium-high heat. Fry eggs, basting occasionally with pan drippings. To make eggs that are browned and crisp around the edges, fry over high heat. Spread hash on a warm platter, top with fried eggs, and sprinkle with parsley. Serve immediately.

Fried Eggs with Sausages

Yield: 4 servings

½ lb Italian sweet sausages
1 Tb vinegar
2 Tb butter
8 eggs
salt and pepper
4 slices bread
1 cup tomato sauce, heated

Fry sausages and drain off fat. Add vinegar to skillet, and cook sausages until liquid evaporates. Drain sausages on paper towels, and cut in slices.

Melt butter in skillet, and fry eggs over medium heat until white is set. Season to taste with salt and pepper.

Toast and butter the bread, then cut slices in half diagonally. On a serving platter, arrange eggs and sausage slices. Cover with hot tomato sauce, and garnish with toast triangles. Serve immediately.

Scrambled Eggs with Chicken Livers and Zucchini (p. 50)

Baked Eggs with Bacon (p. 54)

Piquant Fried Eggs

Yield: 4 servings

2 Tb butter
8 eggs
salt and pepper
4 tsp cider vinegar

Melt butter in a large skillet over low heat, and fry eggs until set to your liking. Remove eggs to a warm platter.

Pour vinegar into skillet, add salt and pepper to taste, and stir with a wooden spoon. Pour vinegar sauce over eggs, and serve immediately.

Baked Tomatoes with Scrambled Eggs

Yield: 4 servings

4 large ripe tomatoes
salt
4 Tb olive oil
6 eggs
2 Tb dry sherry
2 Tb heavy cream
2 heaping Tb grated Parmesan cheese
½ tsp grated lemon peel
pepper
2 Tb butter

Preheat oven to 400°. Rinse tomatoes. Cut a cap from the stem end and reserve. Scoop out tomato seeds and pulp, salt the shells lightly, and invert to drain. Pour 2 tablespoons of oil in a baking dish. Replace caps on tomato shells, and arrange them in the dish. Bake for about 15 minutes, or until tomatoes are cooked but still firm.

Meanwhile, beat eggs and add sherry, cream, grated Parmesan, and lemon peel. Season to taste with salt and pepper. Melt butter in skillet over medium heat, and pour in egg mixture. Turn heat low. Stir constantly and gently until eggs are cooked through, but still moist and creamy in consistency. Remove from heat, and blend in 2 remaining tablespoons of oil. Spoon eggs into tomatoes, set the caps on top, and serve piping hot.

Cherokee Scrambled Eggs

Yield: 4 servings

4 slices bacon
20 wild onions (or 1 bunch scallions)
8 eggs
salt
dash of cayenne pepper

Over very low heat, fry bacon until brown and crisp, then drain on paper towels. Meanwhile, clean and trim onions; chop up both white bulbs and green tops. Pour off all but about 2 tablespoons of bacon fat, raise heat to medium, and sauté onions until limp.

Combine eggs with salt and cayenne to taste, and beat until foamy. Pour eggs into skillet and lower the heat. Stir constantly and gently with a wooden spoon until eggs are cooked through, but still moist and creamy in consistency. Transfer to a warm platter, garnish with crumbled cooked bacon, and serve with a prepared hot pepper sauce.

Chinese Scrambled Eggs

Yield: 4 servings

6 eggs
1 cup rich chicken broth
1 tsp dry sherry (optional)
½ tsp soy sauce
1 Tb cornstarch
½ tsp salt
½ cup water chestnuts, minced
½ cup cooked Smithfield ham, minced
2 Tb oil

Beat eggs together with broth, sherry, soy sauce, cornstarch, and salt. Blend in water chestnuts and ham. In a large skillet, heat oil over medium heat. Pour in egg mixture. Stir constantly and gently with a wooden spoon until eggs just hold together, moist and creamy in consistency.

Country-Style Scrambled Eggs

Yield: 4 servings

8 eggs
salt and pepper
½ tsp rosemary, crushed
½ tsp sage
1 Tb minced parsley
8-oz can tomatoes, drained
3½ Tb butter

Beat eggs together with salt and pepper to taste, plus rosemary, sage, and parsley. Stir in drained tomatoes.

In a large skillet, melt 2 tablespoons of butter over medium heat. Pour in the egg mixture and stir constantly with a wooden spoon.

When eggs just hold together, still moist and creamy in consistency, remove from heat and gently stir in remaining 1½ tablespoons butter. Place eggs on a warm platter and serve immediately.

Scotch Woodcock

Yield: 4 servings

6 eggs
¼ cup milk
pinch of salt
dash of cayenne pepper
1 Tb butter
4 slices buttered toast
4 rolled anchovy fillets
1 Tb minced parsley

Preheat oven to 350°. Break eggs into a bowl, and add milk, salt, and cayenne. Beat lightly with a fork. Melt butter in a skillet over medium heat. When foaming subsides, pour in eggs and lower the heat. Stir constantly and gently with a wooden spoon until eggs just hold together, moist and creamy in consistency.

In a small baking pan, pile eggs on the toast slices. Center a rolled anchovy on each piece. Place in oven until hot, sprinkle with parsley, and serve immediately.

Scrambled Eggs with Cheddar Cheese

Yield: 4 servings

8 eggs
½ cup light cream
salt and pepper
1 cup grated cheddar cheese
2 Tb butter

Beat eggs together with cream and salt and pepper to taste. Blend in cheese.

In a large skillet, melt the butter over medium heat. Pour in egg mixture and lower the heat. Stir constantly and gently with a wooden spoon until eggs just hold together, still moist and creamy in consistency. Serve immediately.

Scrambled Eggs with Chicken Livers and Zucchini

Yield: 4 servings

2 Tb oil
2 small zucchini, sliced thin
2 Tb tomato sauce
¼ lb chicken livers, chopped
5 Tb butter
salt
8 eggs
dash of paprika
4 Tb heavy cream
4 slices toasted bread

In a saucepan, heat oil and sauté zucchini. Add tomato sauce and cook briefly. Sauté chicken livers in 1 tablespoon of butter with a little salt.

Break eggs into a bowl, season with salt to taste and paprika, and beat lightly with a fork. Melt half the remaining butter in skillet over medium heat. When foaming subsides, pour in eggs and lower the heat. Stir constantly and gently with a wooden spoon until eggs are cooked through, but still moist and creamy in consistency. Remove skillet from the heat and stir in remaining butter, cut in small pieces, and heavy cream. Place scrambled eggs on toast slices, and top with sautéed livers and zucchini.

Scrambled Eggs with Cream Cheese and Chives

Yield: 4 servings

8-oz package cream cheese with chives (at room temperature; or plain cream cheese blended with ½ tsp chopped chives)
8 eggs
salt and pepper
2 Tb butter
chopped chives

Cut cream cheese into small pieces, and let soften at room temperature. Beat eggs together with salt and pepper to taste.

In a large skillet, melt butter over medium heat. Pour in the egg mixture, stir in cream cheese, and lower the heat. Stir constantly and gently with a wooden spoon until eggs just hold together, still moist and creamy in consistency. Garnish with chopped chives and serve immediately.

Parmesan Eggs en Cocotte (p. 58)

Scrambled Eggs with Mushrooms

Yield: 4 servings

3 Tb butter
1 cup sliced fresh mushrooms
2 Tb minced parsley
8 eggs
½ cup light cream
salt and pepper

In a large skillet, melt 2 tablespoons of butter over medium heat, and sauté mushrooms until tender. Stir in parsley, and cook for another minute. Beat eggs together with light cream and salt and pepper to taste.

Melt remaining tablespoon of butter in skillet. Pour in egg mixture, and lower the heat. Stir continuously and gently with a wooden spoon until eggs just hold together, still moist and creamy in consistency.

Scrambled Eggs with Peas, Chinese Style

Yield: 4 servings

10-oz package frozen peas
8 eggs
½ cup chicken broth
salt and pepper
1 Tb soy sauce
1 Tb dry sherry
2 Tb oil

Prepare frozen peas according to package directions, but cook for 2 minutes only. Drain well. Beat eggs together with broth, salt and pepper to taste, soy sauce, and sherry.

In a large skillet, heat oil over medium heat. Pour in egg mixture, then gently blend in peas. Stir constantly and gently with a wooden spoon until eggs just hold together, still moist and creamy in consistency.

Scrambled Eggs with Sausages

Yield: 4 servings

6 to 8 breakfast sausages
1 medium-size onion, chopped
8 eggs
2 Tb minced parsley
salt and pepper
2 Tb oil

In a skillet, brown sausages; then drain them on paper towels, and chop coarse. Pour off all but 1 tablespoon of fat from skillet, and sauté onion until tender. Beat eggs, stirring in parsley and salt and pepper to taste. Then stir in sausage and onion.

In a large skillet, heat oil over medium heat. Pour in egg mixture, and lower the heat. Stir constantly and gently with a wooden spoon until eggs just hold together, still moist and creamy in consistency. Serve immediately.

Baked and Poached Eggs

BAKED EGGS AND EGGS EN COCOTTE

An attractive and convenient oven-to-table way of preparing and serving eggs is to bake them in multiple batches in a large casserole, or else singly in individual porcelain ramekins or the chunkier old-fashioned custard cups. Shirred eggs are one kind of egg dish prepared in this latter way—*en cocotte*—baked in buttered ramekins or larger shallow casseroles. Eggs done in this style are often cooked on a bed of puréed vegetables such as spinach, peas, or mushrooms, which helps assure slow, moist cooking conditions to enhance their flavor and consistency. Eggs baked in individual cups or small casseroles should require about 8 to 10 minutes' cooking time; large casseroles, 12 to 15 minutes, on the average.

To keep the surface of baked eggs from becoming tough and chewy, they should first be lightly moistened with some cream, melted butter, broth, or some sort of sauce. This moist coating will ensure tender, rather than rubbery, baked eggs. Another desirable method of baking eggs individually is to immerse the cups or small casseroles in a gently simmering water bath, either on top of the stove or in a moderate oven. This method of slow cooking will also guarantee nicely done and flavorsome egg dishes.

Baked Eggs Florentine

Yield: 4 servings

1 lb fresh spinach (or 10-oz package frozen
  chopped)
salt and pepper
dash of nutmeg, freshly ground
4 Tb heavy cream
4 tsp butter
4 slices cooked ham (or prosciutto)
4 eggs

Wash and cook spinach, drain well and chop, then purée in a blender or food processor. Stir in salt and pepper to taste, nutmeg, and 2 tablespoons of heavy cream.

Preheat oven to 400°. Melt 1 teaspoon of butter in each of 4 small baking cups. Divide half the spinach among the cups, spreading a layer in each. Place a slice of ham in each cup, then cover with remaining spinach. Make a depression in the center of each cup, and break an egg into it. After sprinkling eggs with a little salt and pepper, divide remaining cream among the cups. Bake for 10 minutes, or until eggs are set.

Baked Eggs Piedmontese

Yield: 4 servings

2 lb potatoes
¾ cup grated Parmesan cheese
6 Tb butter
¾ cup milk
salt and pepper
8 eggs
8 anchovy fillets

Scrub potatoes and boil them, unpeeled, until tender. Peel potatoes while still hot and mash, or purée them in a food processor or blender. Add grated Parmesan cheese, 3 tablespoons of butter, milk, and salt and pepper to taste. To dry the mixture, place in a saucepan over low heat for a few minutes, stirring constantly.

Preheat oven to 400°. Butter a heatproof serving dish, and spread the potato mix in it. With the back of a tablespoon, make 8 indentations in its surface; place 1 egg white in each. Put each egg yolk in a separate saucer and place in oven for about 10 minutes, or until egg white has set. Remove from oven, then carefully slide a yolk over each egg white and top with an anchovy fillet. Return baking dish to oven for a few minutes, just until yolk is heated through. Serve piping hot.

Baked Eggs with Bacon

Yield: 4 servings

4 Tb butter, melted
8 slices bacon
8 eggs
salt

Preheat oven to 350°. Divide half the butter among 4 small baking dishes.

Sauté bacon, drain it on paper towels, and place 2 slices in each baking dish. Break 2 eggs into each dish, and season with salt. Pour remaining butter over egg yolks. Bake for about 10 minutes, or until eggs are set. Serve immediately.

Baked Eggs with Italian Ham

Yield: 4 servings

2 cups Béchamel Sauce (see Index)
4 slices Italian ham (prosciutto)
8 eggs
8 Tb grated Parmesan cheese
salt and pepper
4 tsp butter

Preheat oven to 400°. Pour Béchamel Sauce into 4 small ovenproof casseroles, and place a ham slice in each. Break 2 eggs over each slice of ham, and sprinkle each egg with 1 tablespoon of grated Parmesan. Season to taste with salt and pepper, and dot each egg with ½ teaspoon of butter. Bake for 10 minutes, or until eggs are set.

Frothy Baked Eggs (p. 60)

Eggs in Bread Cups (p. 57)

Baked Eggs with Mozzarella and Tomato Sauce

Yield: 4 servings

¾ cup tomato sauce
8 eggs
salt and pepper
8 oz mozzarella cheese, diced
8 rolled anchovy fillets

Preheat oven to 350°. Generously butter 8 small baking cups, and place a heaping tablespoon of tomato sauce in each. Break an egg into each cup, sprinkle with salt and pepper to taste, and top with diced cheese. Place a rolled anchovy fillet in the center and bake for about 15 minutes, or until eggs are set and cheese is melted and bubbly.

Baked Eggs with Mustard

Yield: 4 servings

¾ cup grated Parmesan cheese
8 eggs
⅔ cup heavy cream
1 tsp dry mustard
salt and pepper
1 Tb butter

Preheat oven to 350°. Generously butter a heatproof serving dish, dust with a couple tablespoons of grated Parmesan, and carefully break eggs into the greased dish.

In a bowl, combine heavy cream, mustard, salt and pepper to taste, and remaining cheese. Pour this mixture over eggs, and dot with tablespoon of butter cut in small pieces. Bake for 15 minutes, or until egg whites are set but not browned.

Baked Eggs in Tomato Cups

Yield: 4 servings

4 large tomatoes
salt
4 Tb minced parsley
1 garlic clove, crushed
4 Tb grated Parmesan cheese
10 tsp butter
1 cup soft bread crumbs
8 eggs

Preheat oven to 375°. Cut tomatoes in half horizontally, scoop out their seeds and pulp, salt tomato shells lightly, and invert them to drain.

In a small bowl, combine parsley, garlic, and grated Parmesan. Divide the mixture among the 8 shells, and place ½ teaspoon of butter in each shell. Melt 2 remaining tablespoons butter, then toss bread crumbs in it to toast lightly.

Break an egg into each tomato cup, and top with bread crumbs. Bake for 10 minutes, or until eggs are set. Serve immediately.

Baked Egg Sandwiches

Yield: 4 servings

8 slices toast
4 slices mozzarella cheese
4 slices cooked ham (or prosciutto)
2 Tb olive oil
4 eggs
salt and pepper

Preheat oven to 400°. Arrange 4 slices of toast in greased baking pan. Place mozzarella slice on each, top with slice of ham, and cover with remaining toast slices.

In a skillet, heat olive oil over medium heat, and fry eggs on one side. Place a fried egg on each sandwich, sprinkle with pan drippings, and season to taste with salt and pepper. Bake for 15 minutes, or until mozzarella has melted.

Eggs in Bread Cups

Yield: 4 servings

8 small round rolls
4 tsp butter
1 Tb white vinegar
8 eggs
⅔ cup Béchamel Sauce, heated (see Index)
⅓ cup grated Swiss cheese
1 tsp paprika

Cut a cap from the top of each roll and remove soft centers. Spread ½ teaspoon butter in each of the hollowed rolls, then toast them lightly and keep warm.

In a saucepan, bring a quart of water with the vinegar to a gentle boil. Break eggs, one at a time, into a saucer and slide them very gently into boiling water. Then simmer 3 minutes, or until set. Remove with a slotted spoon, trim the whites if necessary, and place an egg in each toasted roll.

Add grated cheese to the warmed Béchamel Sauce, and stir well. Pour sauce uniformly over the filled rolls, sprinkle with paprika, and serve immediately.

Eggs Benedict

Yield: 4 servings

2 Tb butter
8 slices cooked ham (or Canadian bacon)
1 Tb vinegar
4 English muffins
8 eggs
2 cups Hollandaise Sauce, heated (see Index)

In a skillet, melt butter and sauté ham. Fill a large saucepan with water, bring to a boil, and add vinegar. Lower the heat, and keep water gently simmering.

Meanwhile, split open the English muffins, toast lightly and butter them, place a slice of ham on each, and keep warm. Break eggs, one at a time, into a saucer and slide them gently into simmering water. Poach each egg for 3 minutes, or until set, and remove with a slotted spoon. Set an egg on each muffin half, and pour Hollandaise Sauce evenly over all. Serve immediately.

Eggs en Cocotte with Mushrooms

Yield: 4 servings

butter
8 small slices Italian bread
8 mushroom caps
4 anchovy fillets
8 eggs
4 tsp butter
salt and pepper
boiling water

Preheat oven to 425°. Butter 8 small baking cups. Butter bread, and put 1 slice in each cup.

Clean and slice mushroom caps. Cut anchovies in half. Break an egg into each baking cup, divide sliced mushrooms among the cups, and top each with an anchovy half. Dot each cup with ½ teaspoon of butter, and season to taste with salt and pepper.

Set cups in a baking pan. Fill pan with enough boiling water to reach halfway up the sides of the cups. Bake for about 10 minutes, or until eggs are set. Remove cups from water and dry, set 2 on each plate, and serve immediately.

Parmesan Eggs en Cocotte

Yield: 4 servings

1 cup milk
4 rounded Tb grated Parmesan cheese
salt and pepper
1 tsp grated lemon peel
4 eggs
butter
boiling water

Preheat oven to 375°. Mix milk, grated Parmesan, salt and pepper to taste, and grated lemon peel. Distribute the mixture evenly among 4 small baking cups. Carefully break 1 egg into each cup. Dot eggs with butter.

Set cups in a baking pan. Fill pan with enough boiling water to reach halfway up the sides of the cups. Bake for 10 minutes, or until eggs are set. Remove cups from water and dry, set each on a plate, and serve immediately.

Flemish Eggs

Yield: 4 servings

4 small leaves Belgian endive
salt
4 Tb butter
⅓ cup Béchamel Sauce (see Index)
8 eggs
6 Tb grated Gruyère cheese

Preheat oven to 375°. Clean the endive, pat dry with paper towels, and tear into bite-size pieces. Sprinkle lightly with salt. Melt butter in a small skillet, and sauté endive very briefly over medium heat. Add Béchamel Sauce, stirring to blend well.

Butter 4 small baking dishes very lightly, and divide the sauce evenly among them. Gently break 2 eggs into each dish and sprinkle with Gruyère. Bake for 10 minutes, or until eggs are set and cheese is bubbly. Serve immediately.

58

Frothy Baked Eggs

Yield: 4 servings

8 eggs
salt
8 heaping Tb grated Parmesan cheese
8 Tb heavy cream

Preheat oven to 400°. Separate eggs, placing each yolk in an individual small saucer and all the whites in a deep bowl. Beat whites until thickened. Add salt to taste, and continue beating until stiff moist peaks form. Fold in grated Parmesan.

Generously butter 8 small baking cups, and divide beaten egg whites among them, reserving 8 heaping tablespoons. Make a depression in the center of the egg white in each baking cup, and gently slide an egg yolk into the well. Pour a tablespoon of heavy cream over each yolk, and cover with a heaping tablespoon of reserved egg white. Bake for about 10 minutes, or until eggs are set and light golden brown. Set 2 baking cups on each plate, and serve immediately.

Piquant Eggs en Cocotte

Yield: 4 servings

3 Tb red wine vinegar
8 eggs
8 slices firm-textured white bread
1 heaping Tb capers
1 Tb dry mustard
dash of salt
¼ cup minced parsley
4 Tb olive oil

Fill a large saucepan with water, bring to a boil, and add vinegar. Lower the heat, and keep water at a gentle simmer. Break eggs, one at a time, into a saucer and slide them gently into simmering water. Poach each egg for 3 minutes, or until set, and remove with a slotted spoon. Dip them briefly in a bowl of cold water, then place them in a large shallow pan filled with tepid water to a depth of about 2 inches.

Warm 8 small baking cups in the oven or in a pan of hot water. With a biscuit cutter or water glass, cut circles of bread to fit the top of baking cups. Toast the bread to a rich dark brown.

Mince the capers. Mix mustard with 2 remaining tablespoons of vinegar and dash of salt, stirring until smooth. Add parsley, capers, and olive oil, then blend well. Lift eggs from warm water and drain. Trim the egg whites, if necessary, with a biscuit cutter or downturned water glass, and slide eggs into baking cups. Divide sauce among cups, and cover with a toasted bread round.

Egg and Artichoke Pies

Yield: 4 servings

3 Tb lemon juice (or white vinegar)
4 medium-size artichokes
6 eggs
salt and pepper
all-purpose flour
½ cup oil

In a bowl, add lemon juice (or vinegar) to 4 cups of cold water. Clean and trim artichokes. Discard the stems and tough outer leaves. Cut artichokes in thin slices, and drop immediately into acidy water.

Separate 1 egg, and beat the white until stiff. Beat egg yolk, and season with salt and pepper. Fold egg white gently into yolk. Drain artichokes and pat dry with paper towels. Dredge lightly in flour and dip in egg.

Preheat oven to 350°. Heat oil in skillet over medium-high heat, and fry artichokes quickly until golden brown and crunchy. Drain them on paper towels and divide evenly in 4 small, well-buttered baking dishes. Beat remaining eggs together with salt and pepper, and divide among baking dishes. Bake for 10 minutes, or until eggs are puffed and golden brown.

Baked Potatoes with Egg Filling

Yield: 4 servings

4 large baking potatoes
4 tsp butter
salt and pepper
4 eggs
4 tsp grated Parmesan cheese
4 tsp minced chives (or scallion tops)

Preheat oven to 350°. Scrub potatoes well, wrap them in aluminum foil, and bake for about 1 hour, or until fork-tender. Remove from oven, then increase heat to 400°.

Open the foil without unwrapping the potato. Cut a cap from the top, and scoop out a few tablespoonfuls from the center, leaving a thick shell. In each shell place ½ teaspoon of butter and a dash of salt and pepper. Separate the eggs, and put an egg yolk in each potato shell. Place egg whites in a large bowl. Dot the yolks with remaining butter.

Beat egg whites until stiff peaks form, add grated Parmesan and chives, and spread mixture lightly over egg yolks. Bake potatoes for about 10 minutes, or until eggs are set and golden brown.

POACHED EGGS

Perfect poached eggs are most easily achieved by gently adding the freshest eggs possible to water heated to the barest possible simmer. Vinegar is usually added to the poaching water to firm the white quickly. The eggs may be broken directly into the water close to the surface, or they may be broken into a saucer and slid into the water at surface level. Eggs are poached for 3 to 5 minutes, according to the desired degree of firmness, and then removed from the water with a slotted spoon.

To ensure attractive whites that are not ragged around the edges, eggs may be heat-treated in the shell before poaching. Place room-temperature eggs in a sieve, and lower into vigorously boiling water to cover. Cook very briefly, just long enough to retain the egg shape, or about 8 seconds. Remove eggs from the hot water immediately, and poach as directed above.

Eggs may be poached ahead of time and kept in a bowl of hot water until ready to be used. Reheat them in a bowl of hot (not boiling) water for about 5 minutes, drain, and serve.

Poached Eggs Florentine

Yield: 4 servings

2 lb fresh spinach (or 2 10-oz packages frozen chopped)
3 medium-size potatoes
8 slices bacon
4 tsp butter
1 Tb vinegar
8 eggs
pinch of nutmeg, freshly grated
4 slices Swiss cheese, cut in strips

Rinse fresh spinach thoroughly, cook in a little boiling salted water, drain well, and chop. (Cook frozen spinach according to directions on package.) Scrub potatoes and boil them, unpeeled, until tender. Peel potatoes while still hot and mash, or purée them in a food processor or blender. Cook bacon until brown and crisp, then drain on paper towels.

Combine spinach, potatoes, and butter in a saucepan and place over very low heat to dry the mixture; next, spoon it into a greased heatproof casserole. With the back of a tablespoon, make 8 indentations large enough to hold poached eggs. Fill a large saucepan with water, bring to a boil, and add vinegar. Lower the heat, and keep water gently simmering.

Preheat oven to 400°. Break eggs, one at a time, into a saucer and slide them gently into simmering water. Poach each egg for 3 minutes, or until set, and remove with a slotted spoon to the nests made in the vegetable mixture. Sprinkle with nutmeg, crumble bacon over eggs, and top each egg with cheese. Place in oven for a minute or two, or until the cheese is melted and bubbly. Serve immediately.

Poached Eggs Florentine (p. 62)

Poached Eggs with Asparagus (p. 64)

Poached Eggs
with Asparagus

Yield: 4 servings

8 slices firm-textured white bread
7 Tb butter, melted
1 lb asparagus, cooked (or broccoli)
8 slices fontina (or Swiss) cheese
1 Tb vinegar
8 eggs
8 Tb grated Parmesan cheese

Arrange bread slices in lightly greased baking dish, and sprinkle with half the melted butter. Cut asparagus stalks to fit bread slices, and distribute asparagus equally over the bread. Sprinkle each with a little more melted butter, and keep remaining butter warm. Top asparagus with cheese slices.

Preheat oven to 375°. Fill a large saucepan with water, bring to a boil, and add vinegar. Lower the heat, and keep water gently simmering.

Meanwhile, bake the bread for 5 to 10 minutes, or until cheese is melted. Break eggs, one at a time, into a saucer and slide them gently into simmering water. Poach each egg for 3 minutes, or until set. Remove eggs with a slotted spoon and place one atop each bread square. Pour remaining butter evenly over all, sprinkle with grated Parmesan, and serve immediately.

Poached Eggs
with Peppers

Yield: 4 servings

4 large red or green peppers
2 Tb oil
salt
8 slices bacon
1 Tb vinegar
8 eggs
3½ Tb butter, melted
4 Tb grated Parmesan cheese

Roast peppers by holding them on a long-handled fork directly over high heat on a gas or electric burner. Turn peppers frequently until their skin is blackened and blistered. Under cold running water, peel off burnt skin. Cut peppers in half lengthwise, removing seeds and membrane, and slice them in strips. Dry them carefully, and toss with oil and salt to taste. Cook bacon until lightly browned, and pour off the fat. Drain oil from peppers, and finish cooking the bacon in seasoned oil.

Fill a large saucepan with water, bring to a boil, and add vinegar. Lower the heat, and keep water gently simmering. Break eggs, one at a time, into a saucer and slide them gently into simmering water. Poach each egg for 3 minutes, or until set. With a slotted spoon, remove eggs from water and put them gently in a large bowl filled with cold water.

Preheat oven to 375°. Grease an oblong, heatproof serving dish with half the melted butter, then line it with bacon slices. Drain eggs well, and set an egg on each bacon slice. Top with peppers, and sprinkle with grated Parmesan. Sprinkle with remaining melted butter. Put in oven for 1 or 2 minutes, then serve immediately.

Crêpes, Quiches, and Soufflés

CRÊPES

The word *crêpe* is of French origin and denotes a very thin pancake, exquisitely light in texture when made properly. The only leavening used in the batter is the eggs themselves. The thinness of the pancake is desirable in order to roll them around the countless delicious fillings used with them. There are both hearty main-dish and dessert crêpes, with fillings ranging from meat, vegetables, or seafood to delightful fruit and cream concoctions smothered in sweet sauces.

Kitchen equipment needed for making crêpes is quite simple: mixing bowl; wire whisk or wooden spoon (or else a blender); spatula; and either a special crêpe pan or a rounded-bottom skillet about 6 to 8 inches across. You may have an exclusive, permanently "seasoned" crêpe pan; or instead you

may take a skillet used for other kinds of cooking and season it with some spray shortening, and then some butter or oil, in order to make crêpes with it. You will probably have to discard the first crêpe or two until the pan is adequately seasoned and the right cooking temperature has been achieved.

There are also many curved crêpe griddles available in shops. These are heated to the proper temperature, then dipped in batter and inverted, so that crêpes are actually cooked on the curved outside surface of the griddle. Cooking time for crêpes on a properly prepared surface should be between 30 seconds and 1 minute at most. Crêpes are done when they begin to curl slightly at the edge; they should fall away from the griddle easily when it is inverted.

A smooth crêpe batter is best prepared by hand mixing, since preparation in a blender tends to thicken it, particularly on standing. Batter can be thinned to the proper runny consistency by adding a little milk or water when ready to use.

Breaded Crêpes with Mushrooms

Yield: 4 servings

For crêpes:
2 eggs
⅔ cup milk
¼ tsp salt
½ cup all-purpose flour
oil

Mix eggs, milk, and salt with wire whisk. Add flour, and continue whisking until thoroughly blended. (This step can also be done in blender or food processor.) Let batter stand for 30 minutes.

Heat a 7- or 8-inch crêpe pan or skillet over medium heat, then oil the pan lightly. Pour in ¼ of batter, and tilt pan immediately so that batter completely coats surface. Cook quickly until light brown around edges and dry on top. Turn and lightly brown the other side. Repeat with remaining batter, oiling the pan as necessary. Stack crêpes on a plate. ▷

For filling:

12 oz fresh mushrooms, sliced
3 Tb butter
salt and pepper
1 egg
fine dry bread crumbs
3 Tb grated Parmesan cheese
1 cup Béchamel Sauce, heated (see Index)

Sauté mushrooms quickly in 1 tablespoon of butter. Season with salt and pepper to taste. Divide mushrooms equally among crêpes, then roll crêpes tightly, tucking in their ends so that mushrooms will not spill out.

Beat egg in a shallow plate. Dip crêpes in egg, then roll carefully in bread crumbs to coat well. Melt remaining 2 tablespoons of butter in skillet over medium heat, and brown the crêpes on all sides. Meanwhile, stir grated Parmesan into hot Béchamel Sauce. Place crêpes on a platter, and top with sauce. Serve immediately.

Crêpes with Ham and Mozzarella

Yield: 4 servings

For crêpes:

3 eggs
1 cup milk
¾ cup all-purpose flour
dash of salt
oil

For filling:

2 egg yolks
1½ cups thick Béchamel Sauce (see Index)
8 oz mozzarella cheese, diced
4 slices cooked ham (or prosciutto), chopped
salt and white pepper
¾ cup tomato sauce

Mix eggs, milk, and salt with wire whisk. Add flour, and continue whisking until thoroughly blended. (This step can also be done in blender or food processor.) Let batter stand for 30 minutes.

Heat a 6-inch crêpe pan or skillet over medium heat, then oil the pan lightly. Pour in about 3 tablespoons of batter, and tilt pan immediately so that batter completely coats surface. Cook quickly until light brown around edges and dry on top. Turn and lightly brown the other side. Repeat with remaining batter, oiling the pan as necessary. Stack crêpes on a plate.

In top of double boiler, beat egg yolks and blend in Béchamel Sauce, mozzarella, ham, and salt and pepper to taste. Place over boiling water and, stirring constantly, bring to a simmer. Remove from heat before sauce reaches boiling point.

Preheat oven to 425°. Distribute cheese sauce among crêpes, then roll each crêpe and set in buttered heatproof serving dish. Pour several ribbons of tomato sauce across filled crepes, and bake them for about 10 minutes, or until heated through. Serve immediately.

Egg and Artichoke Pies (p. 61)

Tuna Crêpes

Yield: 4 servings

For crêpes:
2 eggs
⅔ cup milk
¼ tsp salt
½ cup all-purpose flour
oil

For filling:
¼ cup oil
½ cup all-purpose flour
salt and white pepper
1 medium-size onion, minced
2 cups milk
2 Tb dry sherry
2 egg yolks
7-oz can chunk tuna
2 Tb grated Parmesan cheese

Mix eggs, milk, and salt with wire whisk. Add flour and continue whisking until thoroughly blended. (This step can also be done in blender or food processor.) Let batter stand for 30 minutes.

Heat a 6-inch crêpe pan or skillet over medium heat, then oil the pan lightly. Pour in about 3 tablespoons of batter, and tilt pan immediately so that batter completely coats surface. Cook quickly until light brown around edges and dry on top. Turn and lightly brown the other side. Repeat with remaining batter, oiling the pan as necessary. Stack crêpes on a plate.

In a saucepan, combine oil, flour, and salt and pepper to taste. Add onion and stir, cooking for about 2 minutes over medium heat. Gradually blend in milk and cook, stirring constantly, until thick and smooth. Remove from heat. Stir in sherry. Measure and reserve 1 cup of sauce.

Preheat oven to 375°. In a small bowl, beat egg yolks lightly. Blend about ¼ cup of sauce from pan into yolks, then return mixture to saucepan. Heat, stirring constantly, just until it comes to a boil; remove from heat immediately.

Drain and flake tuna; blend into sauce. Spread equal amounts of tuna mixture through center of crêpes. Fold sides toward center and overlap. Arrange in buttered baking dish, top with reserved sauce, and sprinkle with grated Parmesan. Bake for 20 minutes, or until heated through; then serve immediately.

QUICHES

The simplest description of a quiche is "an open-faced cheese pie." It is basically a cheese-flavored egg custard baked in an open pastry shell, combined with a wide variety of possible added ingredients. Among the preferred cheeses to shred or grate for use in quiches are Parmesan, Swiss, Gruyère, and mild cheddar. Tasty additions to the basic cheese custard include various raw or cooked vegetables, bacon or ham, chicken, shellfish, and smoked fish.

While you could use a frozen commercial pastry shell in the following recipes, the tastiest and freshest results doubtless come from preparing your own pastry for the pie shell. Although all these recipes call for a 9- or 10-inch pie shell, it should be remembered you can also make small tart-like quiches for individual servings, instead of the single large pie to be sliced up and served in wedges.

Quiches are properly baked in two (or even three) stages. The basic pie shell must first be partially baked to a light golden hue before the custardy filling is poured in. For this prebaking, the pie shell should be lined with a filler of dried peas or beans or uncooked rice. After 8 or 10 minutes of baking thus, the paper and temporary filler should be removed; then, to ensure crispness, the empty shell can be baked for another few minutes. (Do not allow it to brown, however.)

Satisfactory preliminary baking will keep the pie shell from becoming a soggy mess when filled with the custardy mixture for final baking. A generous sprinkling of shredded or grated cheese over the empty shell during the last few moments of prebaking will give an attractive texture and added tanginess to the finished quiche.

Pie Shell for Quiche

Yield: a 9- or 10-inch pie shell

2 cups all-purpose flour, sifted
½ tsp salt
⅔ cup vegetable shortening, chilled
about ⅓ cup cold water

(For use in the following recipes, it is important that pie pan or quiche pan has a liquid capacity of at least 4 cups. This basic pie shell recipe will yield a generous amount of dough, easily enough for a 9- or 10-inch shell. Leftover pastry can be used for tarts, turnovers, hors d'oeuvres, etc. Dough will keep satisfactorily for 3 or 4 days in refrigerator, or for several weeks in freezer.)

Combine flour and salt in a large bowl. With a pastry blender, mix in shortening until crumbly. Quickly blend in just enough cold water to make a smooth doughy ball. (This step may also be done in a food processor.) Sprinkle dough very lightly with flour, wrap in waxed paper, then chill in refrigerator for an hour or two, or until firm.

On a lightly floured board, roll dough into a round about ⅛ inch thick and 2 inches broader than pie pan or quiche dish to be used. Press dough gently into pan, and crimp or flute the rim. Pierce bottom of pastry several times with a fork. Chill for about 15 minutes.

Line pastry shell with foil, weighted down with dried beans. To partially bake pie shell, bake in preheated 400° oven for 8 minutes to set the pastry. Remove beans and foil, then return shell to oven for 2 more minutes. Cool shell before filling.

Ham and Cheese Quiche

Yield: 6 servings

2 Tb minced onion
1 Tb butter
¾ cup cooked ham, shredded
6 eggs
1 cup heavy cream (or half-and-half)
salt and pepper
¼ tsp dry mustard
dash of nutmeg
¾ cup Swiss cheese, shredded
1 pie shell, partially baked

Preheat oven to 375°. Sauté onion in butter until transparent. Add ham and cook, stirring, for a few minutes. Remove from heat.

Beat eggs together with cream, salt and pepper to taste, mustard, and nutmeg. Gradually blend in ham and cheese. Pour mixture into pie shell. Bake for 30 minutes, or until a knife inserted in the center comes out clean and quiche is puffed and brown.

Mixed Vegetable Quiche

Yield: 6 servings

about 1 lb mixed fresh vegetables, diced (e.g., string beans, broccoli, carrots, celery, zucchini)
4 eggs
1 cup heavy cream (or half-and-half)
salt and pepper
pinch of nutmeg, freshly grated
⅓ cup grated Romano cheese
2 scallions, chopped (including green tops)
1 pie shell, partially baked
1 Tb butter
2 or 3 slices Swiss cheese, cut in thin strips

Steam diced vegetables in a covered metal steamer for about 8 or 10 minutes, or until just beginning to be tender yet still crisp. Set aside to cool briefly. Preheat oven to 375°.

Beat eggs together with cream, salt and pepper to taste, and nutmeg. Mix in steamed vegetables, grated cheese, and chopped scallions, stirring well. Pour mixture into partly baked pie shell, dot with bits of butter, sprinkle with Swiss cheese strips, and bake for about 30 minutes, or until a knife inserted in the center comes out clean and quiche is puffed and beginning to brown.

Mushroom Quiche

Yield: 6 servings

1 scallion, sliced (including green tops)
2 Tb butter
1¼ cups sliced mushrooms, cooked
1 tsp lemon juice
salt and pepper
6 eggs
1 cup heavy cream (or half-and-half)
1 pie shell, partially baked
¼ cup Swiss cheese, shredded

Sauté white scallion slices in 1 tablespoon of butter until just tender. Stir in mushrooms, lemon juice, salt and pepper to taste, and toss lightly. Cook for 2 minutes, stir in green scallion tops, then remove from heat.

Preheat oven to 375°. Beat eggs together with cream and salt and pepper to taste. Drain mushrooms, and gradually blend them into egg mixture. Pour mixture into pie shell. Sprinkle with cheese, and dot with remaining tablespoon of butter. Bake for 30 minutes, or until a knife inserted in the center comes out clean and quiche is puffed and brown.

Mixed Vegetable Quiche (p. 70)

Onion Quiche

Yield: 6 servings

3 cups sliced onions
3 Tb butter
1 Tb all-purpose flour
6 eggs
1 cup heavy cream (or half-and-half)
salt and pepper
¼ tsp dry mustard
pinch of nutmeg, freshly grated
dash of cayenne pepper
½ cup Swiss cheese, shredded
1 pie shell, partially baked

Sauté onions in 2 tablespoons of butter until tender. Sprinkle with flour, blend well, and cook a few more minutes. Onions should be reduced to 1 cup, drained.

Preheat oven to 375°. Beat eggs together with cream, salt and pepper to taste, mustard, nutmeg, and cayenne. Blend in cheese and cup of drained onions. Pour mixture into pie shell. Dot with remaining tablespoon of butter. Bake for 30 minutes, or until a knife inserted in the center comes out clean and quiche is puffed and brown.

Quiche Lorraine

Yield: 6 servings

6 slices bacon
1 medium-size onion, sliced thin
1 pie shell, partially baked
6 eggs
1 cup heavy cream (or half-and-half)
salt and white pepper
pinch of nutmeg, freshly grated
1 cup Gruyère (or Swiss) cheese, shredded

Fry bacon until crisp, then drain on paper towels. Pour off all but 1 tablespoon of bacon drippings, and sauté sliced onion until transparent.

Preheat oven to 375°. Crumble bacon and sprinkle over bottom of pie shell. Beat eggs together with cream. Add salt and pepper to taste and a generous pinch of nutmeg. Blend in Gruyère and sautéed onion. Pour mixture into pie shell. Bake for 30 minutes, or until a knife inserted in the center comes out clean and quiche is puffed and brown.

Seafood Quiche

Yield: 6 servings

1 cup cooked shellfish*
1 scallion, minced (including green tops)
2 Tb butter
2 tsp minced parsley
6 eggs
1 cup heavy cream (or half-and-half)
2 Tb dry sherry
dash of cayenne pepper
½ cup grated Gruyère cheese
1 pie shell, partially baked

Preheat oven to 375°. Chop shellfish in small pieces. Sauté scallion in 1 tablespoon of butter. Add shellfish and parsley, and toss to coat. Cook for 1 minute, then remove from heat.

Beat eggs together with cream, sherry, and cayenne. Blend in shellfish mix and Gruyère. Pour entire mixture into pie shell. Dot with remaining tablespoon of butter. Bake for 30 minutes, or until a knife inserted in the center comes out clean and quiche is puffed and brown.

*Use crabmeat, small shrimp, scallops, or lobster—or a combination of any of these.

Spinach Quiche

Yield: 6 servings

1¼ cups cooked spinach, well drained
1 scallion, minced (including green tops)
2 Tb butter
salt and pepper
pinch of nutmeg, freshly grated
6 eggs
1 cup heavy cream (or half-and-half)
1 pie shell, partially baked
¼ cup grated Swiss cheese

Chop cooked spinach. Sauté scallion in 1 tablespoon of butter for 1 minute, then add spinach and toss to coat. Stir in salt and pepper to taste and a generous pinch of nutmeg. Remove from heat.

Preheat oven to 375°. Beat eggs together with cream and salt and pepper to taste. Gradually blend in seasoned spinach. Pour entire mixture into pie shell. Sprinkle with cheese, and dot with remaining tablespoon of butter. Bake for 30 minutes, or until a knife inserted in the center comes out clean and quiche is puffed and brown.

Crustless Quiche

Yield: 4 to 6 servings

Butter a 9-inch quiche dish or pie plate. Preheat oven to 375°. Prepare any of quiche mixtures in the preceding recipes, and pour into buttered dish or pan. Set dish in a large baking pan and put into the oven. Pour boiling water into baking dish to a depth of ½ inch from top of quiche dish. Bake for 30 minutes, or until a knife inserted in the center comes out clean and quiche is puffed and brown.

Gougère

Yield: 4 servings

2 cups milk
½ cup butter
2 tsp salt
dash of cayenne pepper
2 cups all-purpose flour, sifted
8 eggs
1½ cups Swiss cheese, shredded and loosely
    packed
2 Tb Swiss cheese, finely diced (optional)

Scald milk, let it cool, and strain it into large saucepan. Add butter, salt, and cayenne, then bring to a boil. Add flour all at once. Lower the heat, and beat constantly with wooden spoon until mixture forms a ball that peels away from sides of the pan. Remove from heat. Beat in eggs, one at a time, blending in each egg thoroughly before adding the next. When mixture is satin smooth, stir in cheese.

Preheat oven to 375°. Divide dough in half, and set half aside. With a tablespoon, spoon out pieces of dough about the size of an egg. Place on a buttered baking sheet in a ring, leaving a space at the center about 3 inches across. Then, with a teaspoon, make smaller egg shapes and place these on top of first layer. Make a second gougère with reserved half of dough. The rings may be brushed with a little milk and sprinkled with finely diced cheese. Bake for about 45 minutes, or until gougère is well puffed and deep golden brown.

SOUFFLÉS

The soufflé, the aristocrat of egg cookery, is often considered the prima donna as well. However, even novice cooks armed with the following rules will find this elegant egg dish within their scope.

Soufflés are simply baked combinations of egg yolks, flavored sauce, and beaten egg whites. Cheese, cooked meats, or vegetables—or fruits or sweet flavorings for dessert soufflés—give the dish its character.

The sauce is made first and cooled slightly before adding the egg yolks. It should be cool enough to put your hand comfortably on the bottom of the bowl before the egg whites are folded in. The egg whites should be beaten just before they are to be combined with the sauce.

Start with eggs at least 2 or 3 days old; fresh egg whites won't whip. Egg whites at room temperature will reach peak volume faster than if chilled. A copper bowl is the most suitable container for beating egg whites. Copper reacts with the egg to make the foam more stable. If you use a stainless steel or glass bowl, add a scant ⅛ teaspoon of cream of tartar per egg white to achieve the same effect. Do not use plastic or wooden bowls, since these materials tend to absorb fat and prevent egg whites from whipping.

Hand beating with a large balloon whisk is the fastest and most effective method of encouraging egg whites to peak volume, but beating with an electric mixer is by far the easiest and most popular method. A hand-held beater does a better job than a stationary mixer; just be careful not to overbeat. A blender or food processor will not work satisfactorily here; such machines do not aerate the whites properly.

Beat the whites until they form stiff, but not dry, peaks: they should remain glossy and moist, rising to 6 or 8 times their original volume. Once beaten, they should be folded quickly into the sauce with a spatula. Fold half the whites in thoroughly; fold the other half in lightly, so that the mixture remains puffed and airy. It is all right if some bits of white still show.

Pour the batter gently into a soufflé dish or other straight-sided casserole. Large custard cups can be used for individual servings. The container may be filled to within ½ inch of the top. It is not necessary to grease the baking dish, though a coating of butter dusted with flour, grated cheese, or bread crumbs will add texture and flavor.

Bake the soufflé on a rack in the middle level of a preheated moderate oven. Do not open the oven door for *at least the first 25 minutes of baking time.* The soufflé is done when it is puffed and brown and quivers slightly when the container is moved gently back and forth. If you prefer a dry soufflé, leave it in the oven a few minutes longer.

Finally, the serving time is crucial. Rush the finished dish to the table and serve immediately by gently breaking the soufflé into portions with two forks. Spoon out lightly, including top and side crusts and a bit of the creamy center with each serving.

The recipes for this section were developed using large eggs. Be aware that you may get varying results by using medium- or small-size eggs, and some adjustment of quantity may be desirable.

Spinach Soufflé (p. 78)

Chicken Soufflé

Yield: 4 servings

1 cup thick Béchamel Sauce (see Index)
1½ cups cooked chicken, ground
salt and pepper
pinch of nutmeg, freshly grated
5 eggs, separated
1 additional egg white

Butter a 6-cup soufflé dish, and dust it lightly with flour. Heat Béchamel Sauce, and stir in ground chicken. Season to taste with salt and pepper and a dash of nutmeg. Remove from heat, cool slightly, and add egg yolks, one at a time, blending well after each is added. Pour into a large bowl.

Preheat oven to 350°. Beat 6 egg whites until they form stiff moist peaks. Gently fold egg whites into chicken mixture. Pour into buttered soufflé dish, then bake for about 40 minutes, or until soufflé is puffed and golden brown.

Fontina Soufflé

Yield: 4 servings

¼ cup butter
¼ cup all-purpose flour
1½ cups hot milk
salt and pepper
dash of cayenne pepper
2 cups grated Fontina (or Gruyère) cheese
4 eggs, separated

Melt butter over low heat. When hot and bubbly, add flour and blend thoroughly with wooden spoon. (Do not allow mixture to brown.) Add hot milk, stirring constantly to keep lumps from forming. Season to taste with salt, pepper, and cayenne. Add grated cheese, stirring until sauce is thick and smooth. Remove from heat and cool slightly.

Beat egg yolks, and add them to cheese sauce, blending thoroughly. Pour mix into a large bowl.

Preheat oven to 300°. Beat egg whites until they form stiff moist peaks. Add a few tablespoons of egg white to cheese sauce. Gently fold in remaining egg whites. Pour into ungreased 6-cup soufflé dish. With a teaspoon, make a concentric groove about 1½ inches deep a little more than an inch inside rim of the dish. Bake for 1 hour and 15 minutes, or until soufflé is puffed and golden brown.

Green Bean Soufflé

1 lb green beans   *Yield: 4 servings*
3 Tb butter
3 Tb all-purpose flour
1½ cups hot milk
salt and pepper
pinch of nutmeg, freshly grated
2 Tb grated Parmesan cheese
4 eggs, separated
2 additional egg whites

Trim and wash beans, then cook until well done. Purée cooked beans in blender or food processor. Butter a 6-cup soufflé dish, and dust it lightly with flour.

Melt butter over low heat. When hot and bubbly, add flour and blend thoroughly with wooden spoon. (Do not allow mixture to brown.) Add hot milk, stirring constantly to keep lumps from forming. Season to taste with salt and pepper and a dash of nutmeg, stirring until sauce is thick and smooth. Add grated Parmesan and bean purée, then blend

▷

well. Remove from heat, and pour into a large bowl. Cool slightly. Add egg yolks, one at a time, beating constantly.

Preheat oven to 375°. Beat 6 egg whites until they form stiff moist peaks. Stir about 3 tablespoons of egg whites into purée mixture. Gently fold in remaining egg whites. Pour into buttered soufflé dish, and bake for 35 to 40 minutes, or until soufflé is puffed and golden brown.

Ham and Cheese Soufflé

Yield: 4 servings

¾ cup grated Swiss cheese
¼ cup minced cooked ham
¼ cup minced Italian ham (prosciutto)
1 cup thick Béchamel Sauce (see Index)
4 eggs, separated
salt and white pepper
pinch of nutmeg, freshly grated

Generously butter a 6-cup soufflé dish. Preheat oven to 375°. Next combine cheese, cooked ham, prosciutto, and the Béchamel Sauce. Add egg yolks, one at a time, blending well. Season generously with salt and pepper to taste and nutmeg.

Beat egg whites until they form stiff moist peaks. Fold half the whites into yolk mixture, blending well. Fold in remaining egg whites very lightly. Pour mix into buttered soufflé dish, and bake for 40 minutes, or until soufflé is puffed and golden brown.

Parmesan Soufflé

Yield: 4 servings

2 cups grated Parmesan cheese
¼ cup butter
¼ cup all-purpose flour
1½ cups hot milk
salt and pepper
pinch of nutmeg, freshly grated
4 eggs, separated

Generously butter a 6-cup soufflé dish, and dust it lightly with a little grated Parmesan.

In a saucepan, melt butter over low heat and add flour, blending thoroughly with wooden spoon. Cook for 3 or 4 minutes. (Do not allow mixture to brown.) Add hot milk, stirring constantly to keep lumps from forming. Season to taste with salt, pepper, and nutmeg. Remove from heat and cool slightly. Add rest of grated Parmesan to warm sauce, stirring continually until it melts. Add egg yolks, one at a time, beating constantly.

Preheat oven to 375°. Beat egg whites until they form stiff moist peaks. Gently fold egg whites into cheese mixture. Pour into buttered soufflé dish, and bake for 30 to 45 minutes, or until soufflé is puffed and golden brown.

Salmon Soufflé

Yield: 4 servings

¼ cup butter
¼ cup all-purpose flour
7¾-oz can salmon
¾ tsp dry mustard
salt
dash of cayenne pepper
1 cup hot milk
6 eggs, separated
1 Tb minced parsley

Butter an 8-cup soufflé dish, and dust it lightly with flour. Drain and flake salmon.

In a saucepan, melt butter over low heat, then add flour, mustard, salt to taste, and cayenne, blending thoroughly with wooden spoon. Cook for 3 or 4 minutes. (Do not allow mixture to brown.) Gradually add milk, stirring constantly to keep lumps from forming. Remove from heat and pour into large bowl. Stir a little of this sauce into egg yolks, blending thoroughly; then gradually pour yolk mixture into cream sauce, stirring constantly. Blend in salmon and parsley.

Preheat oven to 350°. Beat egg whites until they form stiff moist peaks. Gently fold egg whites into salmon mixture. Pour into buttered soufflé dish, and bake for about 45 minutes, or until soufflé is puffed and golden brown.

Spinach Soufflé

Yield: 4 to 6 servings

1 lb fresh spinach, washed and trimmed
5 Tb butter
fine bread crumbs
3 Tb all-purpose flour
1 cup hot milk
salt and pepper
pinch of nutmeg, freshly grated
3 Tb grated Parmesan cheese
2 slices lean cooked ham, minced very fine
3 eggs, separated
3 additional egg whites

Cook well-rinsed spinach in a little lightly salted boiling water. Drain, squeeze dry, and chop very fine (or purée in a blender). Butter a 6-cup soufflé dish, and sprinkle lightly with fine dry bread crumbs to add texture; refrigerate prepared dish till needed. Preheat oven to 375°.

Over low heat, melt 4 tablespoons of butter in a skillet or shallow saucepan. (Do not let it brown.) When hot enough, remove briefly from heat to add flour and blend thoroughly with a wooden spoon. Add hot milk and return to low heat, stirring or whisking briskly to keep lumps from forming. Season to taste with salt, pepper, and nutmeg, and continue stirring until sauce is thick and smooth. Blend in well the grated Parmesan spinach, and ham, then cook for another few minutes. Remove from heat, and pour into a large bowl to cool slightly. Add egg yolks one at a time, beating or whisking constantly. Add another light pinch of salt.

Beat all the egg whites until they form stiff moist peaks. First stir a few tablespoons of beaten egg whites into spinach mixture, then gently fold in the remainder. Pour mixture into buttered soufflé dish and level off, then bake for about 30 to 40 minutes, or until soufflé is puffed and rich golden brown.

Index of Recipes by Category

Egg-Based Sauces 12
Aioli (Blender) 12
Béarnaise 12
Béchamel 13
Hollandaise 13
Mousseline 13
Mayonnaise 13
Mayonnaise (Blender) 14
Swedish Egg Sauce 14
Tartar Sauce 14
Egg Soups 16
Chicken Soup Pavia Style (Zuppa Pavese) 16
Cornmeal Egg White Soup 16
Egg and Cheese Dumpling Soup 17
Egg Drop Soup 17
Egg Toast Broth 17
Greek Egg Soup (Avgolemono) 18
Mille-Fanti 18
Onion Soup with Eggs 18
Roman Consommé with Egg Ribbons (Stracciatella) 18
Rolled Crêpes in Broth 20
Spanish Egg Soup 20
Sauced Eggs and Other Dishes 21
Broccoli with Egg Sauce 21
Egg and Cheese Pie 21
Egg Fritters 22
"Eggs in Hell" 22
Eggs Forester Style 24
Hunters' Eggs 24
Mexican Eggs 24
Marie's Peppers and Eggs 25
Piperade 25
San Francisco Eggs and Hamburger 25
Scotch Eggs 26
Strata 26
French Toast 26
Zucchini Veneto Style 26
Soft-, Medium-, and Hard-Cooked Egg Dishes 28
Eggs Cooked in the Shell 28
Soft-Cooked Eggs with Toast Fingers 28
Medium-Hard Eggs with Bacon 29
Medium-Hard Eggs and Mushrooms on Toast 29
Baked Eggs and Asparagus 30
Creamed Eggs in Patty Shells 30
Curried Eggs 30
Eggs in Gelatin 32
Hard-Cooked Eggs with Green Mayonnaise 32
Hard-Cooked Eggs in Tuna Sauce 33
Lemon Stuffed Eggs 33
Mustard Deviled Eggs 33
Stuffed Eggs with Mushrooms and Tuna 34
Stuffed Tomatoes 34
Omelets and Frittatas 36
Omelets 36
Fluffy Omelet 36
Fresh Tomato Omelet 37
Ham Omelet 37
Mozzarella Omelet 37
Omelet with Croutons 38
Saffron Omelet 38
Frittatas 40
Asparagus and Mushroom Frittata 40
Chinese Frittata 41
Ham and Tomato Frittata 41
Hearty Scallion Frittata 41
Noodle and Sausage Frittata 42
Pepper and Onion Frittata 42
Rice Frittata 42
Savory Chicken Frittata 44
Spinach Frittata 44
Tomato and Mozzarella Frittata 45
Tuna Frittata 45
Fried and Scrambled Eggs 46
Fried Eggs Neapolitan 46
Fried Eggs and Hash 46
Fried Eggs with Sausages 46
Piquant Fried Eggs 48
Baked Tomatoes with Scrambled Eggs 48

Cherokee Scrambled Eggs 48
Chinese Scrambled Eggs 49
Country-Style Scrambled Eggs 49
Scotch Woodcock 49
Scrambled Eggs with Cheddar
  Cheese 50
Scrambled Eggs with Chicken Livers
  and Zucchini 50
Scrambled Eggs with Cream Cheese
  and Chives 50
Scrambled Eggs with Mushrooms 52
Scrambled Eggs with Peas, Chinese
  Style 52
Scrambled Eggs with Sausages 52
Baked and Poached Eggs 53
Baked Eggs and Eggs en Cocotte 53
Baked Eggs Florentine 53
Baked Eggs Piedmontese 54
Baked Eggs with Bacon 54
Baked Eggs with Italian Ham 54
Baked Eggs with Mozzarella and
  Tomato Sauce 56
Baked Eggs with Mustard 56
Baked Eggs in Tomato Cups 56
Baked Egg Sandwiches 57
Eggs in Bread Cups 57
Eggs Benedict 57
Eggs en Cocotte with Mushrooms 58
Parmesan Eggs en Cocotte 58
Flemish Eggs 58
Frothy Baked Eggs 60

Piquant Eggs en Cocotte 60
Egg and Artichoke Pies 61
Baked Potatoes with Egg Filling 61
Poached Eggs 62
Poached Eggs Florentine 62
Poached Eggs with Asparagus 64
Poached Eggs with Peppers 64
Crêpes, Quiches, and Soufflés 65
Crêpes 65
Breaded Crêpes with Mushrooms 65
Crêpes with Ham and Mozzarella 66
Tuna Crêpes 68
Quiches 69
Pie Shell for Quiche 69
Ham and Cheese Quiche 70
Mixed Vegetable Quiche 70
Mushroom Quiche 70
Onion Quiche 72
Quiche Lorraine 72
Seafood Quiche 72
Spinach Quiche 73
Crustless Quiche 73
Gougère 73
Soufflés 74
Chicken Soufflé 76
Fontina Soufflé 76
Green Bean Soufflé 76
Ham and Cheese Soufflé 77
Parmesan Soufflé 77
Salmon Soufflé 78
Spinach Soufflé 78